Scooter Mania!

Eric Dregni

MBI Publishing Company

First published in 1998 by MBI Publishing Company, 729
Prospect Avenue, PO Box 1, Osceola, WI
54020-0001 USA.

MBI Publishing Company books are also available at
discounts in bulk quantity for industrial or sales-
promotional use. For details write to Special Sales
Manager at Motorbooks International Wholesalers &
Distributors, 729 Prospect Avenue, PO Box 1, Osceola,
WI 54020-0001 USA.

Library of Congress Cataloging-in-Publication Data

Dregni, Eric
        Scooter mania/ Eric Dregni.
            p. cm.
        Includes index.
        ISBN 0-7603-0446-7 (pbk.)
        1. Motor scooters--History. 2. Motorcycling--
        History. I. Title.
TL450.D73   1998
629.227'5' 09--dc21   98-29634
                                        CIP

On the front cover:
Nothing like zipping down an alley on a cold January day in Minneapolis near Loring Park. This mod steed is a tricked out Lambretta Turismo Veloce 175 Series II with extra mirrors and lights attached to the roll bar. Mod models who graciously got gussied up for the advancement of scooterdom are Tim Gartman and Jessika Madison. Tony Nelson

On the frontispiece:
"Learn a new definition of fun," urged a 1960 Super Eagle brochure, and what better way than with telescopic front forks, 12-volt electrics, and "streamlined" style. A buddy seat, roll bar, and chrome doodads have been added to this 1959 model.

On the title page:
With only seven remaining in existence of the 1,200 made, the top-of-the-line Einspurauto *(one-track car) has become one of the most collectable putt-putts for scooter museums across Europe. A marriage of French design by Monsieur Lepoix and German production, the Bastert featured a low center of gravity and offered a smooth ride.*

On the back cover:
Top: Three answers to the question, "what is a scooter?": the French Terrot (left), a restored 125-cc Italian Vespa (center), and the American Salsbury Super-Scooter Model 85 (right). Bottom: Racy women on fast scooters have long been a staple of Italian scooter advertising. Vittorio Tessera archive

Edited by Zack Miller
Designed by Tom Heffron

Printed in Hong Kong through World Print, Ltd.

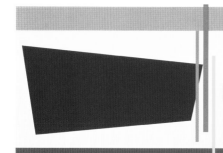

Contents

Acknowledgments

The smirks and sidelong glances when scooters are brought up are enough to plunge any self-respecting writer back into the abyss of waiting tables. I'd like to thank the following people who stood by me and believe that the world will be a better place when everyone knows even more about these two-wheeled wonders: Kris Adams; Ansgar; Bruno Baccari for allowing a scooter amid his motorcycles; Dan Baker and his mint Cushmans; Joe Baker's nuova linea; Stacey Rae Becklund; Alessandra Bonacci for advice on disobeying Roman street signs; Chank's scooter fonts; Guido Delli Pontis' MVs; S. Croce; Roberto Donati and Paperino; Pa Dregni—photo assistant extraordinaire; mon frère Michael Dregni; François-Marie Dumas and the whirlwind tour of Parisian scooterdom; Elio e le Storie Tese; Anna Erba and her Lambrate haven; Giovanni "oregano and basil are enemies" Erba; Erica (with an "a"); Christophe Fresneau for keeping Bernardet scooters on the road; Yves Dumetz; Michel Gagnaires' Vélautos; Didier Ganneau; Tim Gartman; JJ Gauthier for putting up with scooter shoots; Curt Grese's 1951 Eagle; Paolo Giuri for sneaking me into la Piaggio in spite of impending strikes; Bruno Gridel's Skootamotas; Nick "scooters are my life" Hook; Patrick Jones; Karl Hagstrom Miller for advice on sounding important and academic; Tom Houck; Jason Johnson; Jim Kilau for his continual hunt for the most obscure American scooters; Hans Kruger and his scooter Xanadu; Leif Larsen for saving me from computer inferno; Marina "red light, red light, run it!" Leonardi; Herb and Linda Letourneau's Eagles; W. Conrad Link; Jessika Madison—Moddest of Mods; Mao; Mr. Marvelous; Roger McLaren's Model 52; The Minneapolis Police Department—you can insult me but not my Lambretta; Mike Nilles for letting me tap away on his laptop (even if it is Windows); Willy and Sam Niskanen; Lauró Orestano for lending me a Sfera and teaching me to drive like a fearless Italian; John Van Orman for scoping out Salsburys; John "Italia" Perkins; JP Porter for listening to my scooter babble 24 hours per diem; Dott. Pietro Rozza and Christa Solbach of the Vespa Club Rome; Halwart and Mila Schrader for believing in scooters auf Deutschland; Craig at Scooterworks for pushing to get the Vespa back in the United States; Herb Singe and his scooter warehouses; Leon Stevenart; Sven the Cat; Vittorio Tessera and his golden-fleeced Lambretta; Pete "I Don't Know Anything About Scooters" Townshend; Mark Ulves; Becky Wallace and her mod archives; Jürgen Wangermann; Keith and Kim Weeks' Cushmans and Doodlebugs; and Andrea Zanivan for correcting my questionable Italian.
—Eric Dregni

6

In the 20th century, speed has changed the world more than any other concept. Europe is connected to the Americas through jet planes; towns are connected to cities via turbo cars and high-speed trains; and a jaunt to the E-Z Stop takes only minutes thanks to scooters. Distances are no longer an issue, or as Futurist F. T. Marinetti pronounced, "Time and space died yesterday."

Never before in history have humans been as mobile as now. "The wheel is an extension of the foot," according to philosopher Marshall McLuhan. First you crawl, then walk, then scoot. Walking has become obsolete, and scooters have replaced the foot as the basic form of transportation in many cities.

Once we feel how fast we can go, we never want to slow down. Marinetti declared that "the world's magnificence has been enriched by a new beauty; the beauty of speed." This new "invention" spawned steeply banked boardtrack "motordrome" raceways, a.k.a. "murderdromes," in the 1920s, where motorcyclists would break 80 miles per hour—and sometimes their necks too.

With the introduction of the scooter, speed-crazed folks who couldn't afford to hop on souped-up motorcycles to take a spin on the soon-outlawed motordromes were able to fulfill their desire for speed.

Early scooters were crude and often dangerous machines, however. Curious-looking contraptions with spot welds and borrowed lawnmower engines underwent product testing on the unsuspecting general public. *Popular Mechanics* gave a bizarre endorsement to an extremely uncomfortable scooter in 1947 noting that, "One manufacturer bolts the driver's seat directly to the cylinder head by means of extension rods to save space and to reduce weight."

Most of the media, though, didn't hold back when describing these awkward machines. A 1938 *Chicago Daily Times* article about Moto-Scoot pulled no punches, calling them "puddle-jumpers," "vest-pocket motorcycles," and a "powered roller skate." *Life* magazine pooh-poohed the scooter revolution of the 1950s, referring to the mini cycles as "only a tame plaything in the U.S." *Time* magazine provided scooter critics with new insults to hurl in 1967: ". . . because of their blue crash helmets, scooter men endure such other names as 'blister-heads' and 'bubbleheads.'" Scooter designers ignored the criticism, and gave the public the "speed" they wanted.

What non-believers don't understand is that speed is relative. Tourists enjoy high tea on the Concorde, zooming at 600 miles per hour over the ocean; French passengers doze while high-speed

While Piaggio's putt-putts may have revolutionized the two-stroke industry, Zündapp's Bella proved that German engineering could perfect the scooter. With a longer wheelbase and larger 12-inch wheels for more stability, the Bella wasn't so tippy. With a peppy 150-cc or 200-cc engine, touring was par for the course. Rather than copying the Lambretta as NSU did (under license) or the Vespa as everyone else did, Zündapp based its design on the Moto Parilla Levriere.

TGV trains carry them into the Gare de Lyon at 300 kilometers per hour; Ferrari F550 drivers relax to Musak while leaving Fiat 500s breathing their 200-mile-per-hour exhaust. Not so on a scooter. Even a brave Ducati motorcycle rider grows pale when attempting 35-mile-per-hour speeds on a Vespa, all the while dodging bored car drivers busily talking on cell phones, smoking cigarettes, and applying makeup. Handling the mini wheels, the nearly vertical front fork, and the buzzing two-stroke engine tempts the Grim Reaper and brings the rider one step closer to the scooter netherworld.

This semblance of pure speed is what makes riding a scooter such a thrill. As Jean Baudrillard wrote in his book *America*: "Speed creates pure objects. It is itself a pure object, since it cancels out the ground and territorial reference-points . . ." He might as well have been describing a joyride on a 1963 Lambretta TV 175.

With speed comes danger. Early scooters on minuscule wagon wheels were usually targeted as death traps, which is why National Safety Council member General George C. Stewart declared in the 1950s, "I would rather have a 14-year-old child of mine turned loose in traffic with a 10-ton truck than on a scooter."

In spite of helpful warnings from responsible adults, riders' wanderlust threw caution to the wind, and scooters were soon traveling huge distances in the Old and New World. *Popular Science* uncovered some of the pitfalls for putt-putt adventurers in a 1957 article warning, "Dogs are conservative animals easily outraged by the unconventional and will frisk alongside munching at your heels." At the same time the article encouraged scooter folly, "Snow, however, is navigable if you know your stuff." Scooter shortcomings were conveniently overlooked with forgiving text like, "You can see behind simply by turning your head."

The scooter became the dream machine of teenagers, and an economic necessity as a "second car" to suburban families who couldn't afford another set of four wheels. As *Newsweek* wrote in 1956, "Factory hands and white-collar workers plunked wife on the rear seat, baby in a basket on the handlebars, junior on the floor boards and set off on Sunday outings." Once scooterists were mobile, they got the bug for speed and could never go back to walking. Scooter mania had taken over the world.

French, Italian, and American. Three of the coolest scooters ever to hit pavement: the French Terrot with an oversized nose, a restored 125-cc Italian Vespa, and the American Salsbury Super-Scooter Model 85.

Chapter 1 | The Early Years

Cities in the 1800s were in sorry shape. Horses were the mainstay of transportation around the turn of the century, often dropping dead from overexertion during rush hour. When sharpened spurs failed to coax tired steeds, teamsters supposedly would light fires under horses' bellies to urge them up hills. Even so, the sight of the poor beasts collapsing made city dwellers hungry for change. Horse deaths were extremely common. "By the 1880s, New York City was removing 15,000 bodies annually," according to Clay McShane in *Down the Asphalt Path*. "When a horse actually did drop dead, traffic was delayed even more. Sanitation departments took hours, sometimes days, to remove the carcasses."

While environmentalists may look back fondly on the horse-and-buggy days free of pollution, consider the gruesome fact that the manure from these horses averaged one million pounds a day in New York. McShane further enlightens us:

> The Central Park Stable, hardly the largest in New York City, had a 30,000 cubic foot pile of

Designed by Kurt Passow in 1922, the Pawa perhaps ranks more as a motorcycle than scooter, but the extensive floorboards and covered engine still give it some scooter credibility. This photo dates from 1923 with two determined riders heading down the sidewalk. Whoops, forgot to lift the kickstand. François-Marie Dumas archives

manure next to it . . . health officials in Rochester, New York claimed that if all the manure produced in one year by each of that city's horses were gathered in one place, the resulting pile would cover one acre of ground to a height of 175 feet. They claimed that the pile would breed 16 billion flies, each a potential carrier of germs.

Luckily the noble and eccentric Baron Drais of Karlsruhe, Germany, knew that necessity breeds invention and had been hard at work to mobilize the world. He scorned the life of luxury and followed his lust for inventing, unveiling a vehicle that would revolutionize the world in 1813. "He started with the correct notion that a walking man uses up too much energy by throwing about his weight from one foot to the other. How is it possible to keep one's body constantly in the same axis when moving forward?" asked Egon Larsen in *Ideas and Invention*. After he proved to local naysayers that he could easily wheel from Karlsruhe to the neighboring town in less than half the time it takes by foot, he was allowed to patent his velocipede—but only in the province of Baden. His idea was soon copied across France, England, and the United States, where plagiarists avoided paying royalties by hiding behind pseudonyms like "dandy horses," "hobby horses," and "bone shakers." These early bicycles were considered playthings for the wealthy and the

AUTOPEDING

— SOMETHING NEW IN TRANSPORTATION

As Ralph Waldo Emerson said, "Invention breeds invention." Accordingly, the motorscooter was bred from Daimler's motorcycle. But instead of plopping an engine on a bicycle, motorscooter inventors used a child's push toy, the scooter. Many early French motorcycles from the 1910s and the Militaire from Cleveland, Ohio, used a step-through design, avoiding the bulky gas tank between the legs and improving stability.

The Autoped of New York, looking less like a step-through motorcycle than a motorized child's toy, was the first scooter to be built in large numbers; it was available commercially around the country. In fact, after it was imported in 1916, "Autoped" became synonymous for "child's scooter" in Dutch.

Another "ped" followed. In this case it was the Motoped, which set the standard with a 1.5-horsepower engine mounted on the left side of the front wheel, giving the scooter a lean later adopted by Piaggio's Vespa. The "Fred-Flinstone" brakes relied on the magic of shoe leather, one area where the Motoped clearly needed improvement.

The Autoped "Wonder of the Motor Vehicle World" was copied throughout Europe—some licensed and others not—by companies like Krupp in Germany (with a larger 200-cc engine), UK Imperial Motor Industries, and CAS in Czechoslovakia with a 155-cc engine. Interestingly, while bicycles were being banned on many city roads because residents were terrorized by speed, the 1914 Autoped was made for sidewalk use. Even so, ads claimed that the scooter could hit 60 kilometers per hour (while in reality more like 25 kilometers per hour).

butt of working class jokes, especially the "penny-farthings" bikes so called for the uneven relation between the front and the back wheels.

As bicycles became the rage of the rich, Parisian inventor Jean-Joseph Lenoir was building the first internal combustion engine in 1860. Gottlieb Daimler and Nikolas Otto took Lenoir's four-stroke motor to a new level by making it capable of 700 rpm. Then in 1885, Daimler took the next logical step, mounting his engine on a stout velocipede thus creating the first gas-engine-powered motorcycle.

Soon copies of the Autoped were popping up across the United States and Europe, each with minor improvements to the original. Germany had its DKW, Golem, and Megola, and England had its Wilkinson. The English Autoglider De Luxe appeared in 1919, created by Charles Ralph Townsend at Townsend Engineering Co. of Birmingham with a 269-cc Villiers engine mounted on a front 16-inch wheel. The Model A was seatless like the Autoped, but the Model D added a cushioned seat that doubled as suspension. Even though ads claimed top speed was 50 kilometers per hour, bold scooterists claimed to have reached 80 kilometers per hour, although probably down a steep hill.

Both England and the United States had versions of the Neracar (an American design licensed to an English manufacturer) a half-scooter, half-motorcycle hybrid with dual headlamps that was originally intended for women since it had a low center of gravity and dual springs to ease the ride. England then produced the Stafford Mobile Pup in 1919, adding a comfortable seat and wider floorboard. France added class to the original

equation with the beautiful Monet-Goyon Vélauto in 1919 with a wicker seat and some color to the paint scheme. The first Monet-Goyon built in Mâcon, France, was propelled by a 147-cc, 2-horsepower Villiers, followed by the Super Vélauto with 27-cc engine.

Perhaps one of the most important putt-putts to further the cause was the 1919 ABC Skootamota with a 147-cc engine. Built until 1923, the

When the starlet Mistinguett jumped on a Skootamota, the paparazzi were there to splash her mug across Le Miroir, causing a mini revolution for the scooter world. This article announced the formation of Scooter Club de France in 1920 at this rally at Saint-Cloud park. Finally even the Parisian sophisticates could hop on a putt-putt and avoid soiling themselves by scooting right around the horse dung littering the streets of the day. François-Marie Dumas archives

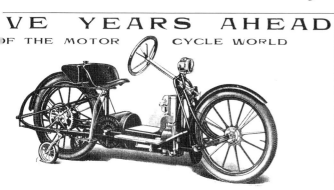

The scooter's identity crisis between being part motorcycle and part automobile stretches to the dawn of scootering when the primordial ooze formed the first putt-putts. "The car on two wheels" notion began with the Militaire (1912 model shown), which came equipped with training wheels lowered from the rear hub to stabilize this E-Z Boy when at a full stop.

In the early 1900s in France, the bicycle was the fad that swept the country. Monet-Goyon tried to invent the new Hula-Hoop by combining the bicycle (le vélo) with an automobile, thus producing the Vélauto. The 1921 Monet-Goyon Vélauto (right) had a 117-cc engine, while the 1922 Monet-Goyon Super Vélauto (left) upped the ante to a 270-cc motor with an air pump to inflate tires around the 16-inch wheels. François-Marie Dumas archives

Skootamota later switched to a 110-cc overhead valve engine with seat on top of the diminutive 8-inch wheels. The forward-looking French received the ABC with open arms and became one of the main markets for engineer Granville Branshaw's design. An early French ad proclaimed that:

> If Madame has to meet a friend at 11 o'clock at the Bois de Boulogne, at noon be at home for lunch, then shop at the big stores downtown, and later in the evening dine with friends in the suburbs. She would never be able to do all this by taking outrageously priced taxis that are impossible to flag down. Knowing this, Madame bought a SKOOTA-MOTA, the woman's machine 'par excellence' which is easy to drive, doesn't demand any mechanical knowledge, and doesn't need a garage.

While most of these early scooters seem primitive compared to today's jetpod styling, the Unibus of Gloucestershire Aircraft Company of Cheltenham,

The Skootamota was created by English engineer Granville Bradshaw with a hefty 147-cc intake-over-exhaust motor. Deemed the perfect mobile for ladies, the Skootamota added a floorboard allowing the latest dresses to be worn without that bothersome bar between the legs. This 1919 Model ABC Skootamota added a leather seat to the basic design put forth by Motoped and Autoped. François-Marie Dumas archives

Townsend Engineering Company of Birmingham, England, cashed in on the first scooter craze with its Autoglider, one of the first scooters to look like the Vespas and Lambrettas cruising the streets today. Charles Ralph Townsend's Model A lacked a seat, but this 1919 De Luxe model added a cushion to make up for the lack of shock. The bulky, front-mounted 269-cc Villiers engine and gas tank balanced the weight of the driver, but made the poor soul inhale its exhaust. François-Marie Dumas archives

England, went beyond just crossing a child's scooter with a motorcycle, and melded not just a motorcycle with a car, but added the third design element: the airplane. With a sleek covered body hiding the dirty engine, the 1920 Unibus finally set the stage and drew the design for scooters to come. While the name would suggest a one-person bus, ad copy claimed that "To see the Unibus is to want one," and called it the "Car on Two Wheels," a motto later taken up by German Maico scooters in the 1950s as "Das Auto auf 2 Rädern."

The early motorscooters were considered mostly a passing fad for the elite. While futuristic brochures may have boasted that soon everyone would save the soles of their shoes by hopping on an Autoped, in reality most folks scrounged to even afford the luxury of a bicycle.

BUILD IT YOURSELF, AT YOUR OWN RISK

The second great scooter boom in America began with do-it-yourselfers. Rather than distributing lower quality scooters to showrooms across the country, many manufacturers opted for mail-order at "only bicycle cost." Renmore of Wabash Avenue in the Windy City offered its Constructa-Scoot: "Just send $29.50 less motor, $59.50 with motor." Others like Zipscoot of Toledo, Ohio, merely offered plans for its "smart looking speedster" with a top speed of 30 miles per hour for only 25 cents. Hmmm . . .

To get their mags to fly off the newsstand, *Popular Mechanics* continually ran plans showing how to build your own putt-putt, "First find an old washing machine motor," get a couple of pine planks, some old wagon wheels, and BINGO! Scraped knees.

In spite of the usual shoddy construction, innovative designs did exist, like that from LeJay Electric Rocket of Minneapolis that peddled blueprints for an electric motor-powered build-your-own scooter in 1939. Today modern scooter companies are again toying with the idea of pollution-free electric motors. Even the European Union is experimenting with renting electric bicycle/scooters in medium-sized cities. Perhaps a look at some old *Popular Mechanics* back issues is in order.

Chapter 2
Buzzcut Years of American Scootering

The Salsbury Motor Glide was born in the back of a heating and plumbing shop in Oakland, California. E. Foster Salsbury had been inspired when he saw Amelia Earhart buzzing around on a Motoped in Burbank. "It got me started thinking about building a real scooter," recalled E. Foster Salsbury in 1992. Pilots helped keep alive the putt-putts from the first scooter wave, because scooters were ideal for zipping down the tarmac to waiting planes. "Even the fast-flying airplane has to rely on the lowly scooter when taxiing into a parking area at the airport," wrote *Popular Mechanics* in 1947. After Salsbury and engineer Austin Elmore pieced together the first Motor Glide in 1936, famous aviator Colonel Roscoe Turner caught a whiff and was hooked. Soon Turner pushed Salsbury scooters

Toward the end of World War II, Lewis Thostenson designed the ultimate spaceship-cum-scooter—the coveted Salsbury Model 85. Debuting in 1946 when the age of the children's motorized putt-putt was over, between 700 and 1,000 Jet Age Salsburys hit the streets of Los Angeles. The Model 85 came in two forms with the same 6-horsepower engines: the Standard and the DeLuxe with the added plexiglass fairing. In spite of its blast-off design, the Model 85 was a cinch to maneuver, "There's no clutch lever, no gear shift . . . Stop and Go pedals are the only controls." E. Foster Salsbury archives

whenever he went on the road with his air show, and proclaimed, "The Salsbury Motor Glide is the greatest woman catcher I have ever seen." Soon, even the likes of Bing Crosby dropped cash for a Motor Glide to pick up chicks.

Apart from being a lady-killer, the 1936 Motor Glide established the "Five Commandments of Scooters," of which all putt-putts carried at least three traits:

1. Motor placed under the rider usually just in front of the rear wheel.
2. Step-through chassis, i.e., no bar between the rider's legs.
3. Covered motor and leg shield, to protect the rider from the elements and to hide the sloppy engine.
4. Minuscule wheels, giving added maneuverability (some would say "instability").
5. Automatic transmission or a clutch and gears controlled by hand levers.

The 1936 Motor Glide wasn't much to look at, but, as scribbled on the back of an early promotional photo from the Salsbury archives, "It worked fine on dry pavement." Despite its primitive appearance, its technological design revolutionized the scooter industry and set the standard for all later scooters.

The 1937 Salsbury Motor Glide was further improved as were the brochures: "Dash hither and yon in gay abandon . . . eases through traffic like an eel. . . . It's as safe as an armchair and as comfortable. . . ." The California-based company, conscious of its image with the jet set, proclaimed its scooter, "an instant hit in the Hollywood movie colony at swanky Palm Springs and gay Florida resorts." Even so, the ground-breaking scooter lacked the style that would be added a decade later, although it did offer a special seat "padded with felt and hair."

In 1938, updates included a revolutionary self-shifting transmission later copied by every scooter manufacturer from Honda to Piaggio. The idea was simple: As the speed of the engine increased, the drive pulley was pushed together, giving a bigger circumference for the belt to ride on and thereby increasing the "gear ratio." Salsbury again changed engine manufacturers—this time to Lauson motors—following previous trials with Evinrude and Johnson, and even rejecting a bid for 1,000 Cushman Husky engines.

This unrestored 1938 Model 50 with Salsbury's special torque converter carried on E. Foster Salsbury's scooter revolution. The little Motor Glide was used for everything from pilot porter to Warner Bros. assistant in Tinseltown to ambulance with a sidecar to carry the patient. It's no wonder the ad copy for this little Salsbury reminisced, "Dash hither and yon in gay abandon . . . learn the difference between GLIDING over city streets and country road and pedaling or 'puddle-jumping.'"

"CUSTER SCOOTER is TOPS," blared ads for the Dayton, Ohio, scooter produced in the late 1930s. This extremely rare 1937 Custer has a minuscule 1.5-horsepower motor, but what it lacks in power it makes up for in the oft-copied teardrop styling. The U.S. military even performed top secret road tests of this petite putt-putt alongside hardier Cushmans and Coopers, but the poor Custer's souped up 2.5-horsepower engine was deemed unworthy to carry the troops to V-Day.

Meanwhile, across town, Salsbury's Motor Glide had spawned competition when Albert G. Crocker received a call from motorcycle mogul Floyd Clymer of Los Angeles to help him hop on the scooter bandwagon. Thus, the Crocker Scootabout was born in the 1930s, adding beautiful Art Deco styling and a two-tone paint scheme—years before the Mods—to this otherwise utilitarian-looking two-wheeler. Salsbury had the jump on the competition, though, and less than 100 Scootabouts were ever built.

To try and extend Salsbury scooter sales into Europe in 1938, an agent headed into the Old Country armed with blueprints and brochures to try and convince foreign manufacturers to sign on the dotted line. E. Foster Salsbury believed that one of the companies was Piaggio. Who knows what would have happened if the Vespa was never conceived and Italy was motorized with Salsburys? Instead, Benito and Adolf spoiled everything.

During World War II, Salsbury pitched into the war effort and worked on experimental wind tunnels to test airplanes. Between 1944 and 1945, Avion Inc., a Los Angeles war material company, bought out Salsbury and moved the new company to Pomona, California. Northrup Aircraft Company bought out Avion in 1946. With all this aviation company involvement, it was no surprise when Northrop introduced the sleekest scooter ever built: the Model 85, in 1946. Engineer Lewis

THE REVOLUTIONARY SALSBURY SUPER-SCOOTER

Thostenson was able to scrounge enough time during the war years to design a Buck Roger's two-wheeler that would hit the showrooms just one year after the war. Finally, Avion scooters changed the name "Motor Glide"—easily confused with Cushman's ubiquitous "Auto Glide"—to just "Salsbury." All the technological stops were pulled out as the new Salsbury Super-Scooter was deemed the "MOST COMPLETELY AUTOMATIC VEHICLE EVER BUILT" by Salsbury ad copy. This two-wheeled marvel featured a special "Straight-Shot" carburetor, torque converter, one-sided front forks (similar to those on airplanes), and, of course, the automatic drive inscribed with new words replacing the clumsy "throttle and brake" with the simpler "stop and go." Unfortunately, the Salsbury Super-Scooter only survived from 1946 to 1949 at which time it was run off the road by the huge American cars of the 1950s.

Powell's Putt-Putts

Deep during the Depression, designers saw the simplicity of Salsbury's Motor Glide. Entrepreneurs such as the Powell brothers, Channing and Hayward, from Los Angeles, pulled out their tool kits and reinvented the scooter. The 2.3-horsepower Lauson engine, with the aid of a centrifugal clutch, could barely push the early Streamliner to 30 miles per hour. In 1940, the Powells turned from mini-scooters to mini-motorcycles, with the punning A-V-8 (Aviate), now a 5-horsepower engine with options like the first scooter push-button start.

Frank Cooper bought some A-V-8s, tattooed his own name on the gas tank, welded a web of metal to the frame, and submitted the "Cooper War Combat Motor Scooter" to the U.S. Army as a scooter ideal for parachuting. While Cooper's scooter impressed the doughboys, his makeshift factory left something to be desired. The contract

The "CHEAPER THAN SHOE LEATHER Auto Glide" was Cushman's debut into the scooter realm. By the time this 1938 Auto Glide hit the pavement, most of the dangerous quirks of the first model no longer spelled certain disaster. Looking through rose-colored glasses at the poky 1-horsepower Cushman engine, ad copy assured that, "Low speed insures safety. Auto-Glide is NOT a 'speed wagon.'"

went to Nebraska's Cushman. Powell's remaining stock was bought out by Clark Engineering in 1942 and re-released as the Victory Clipper and later as the Clark Cyclone.

By 1945, Powell was able to stop making rockets and shells, and re-enter the scooter biz with the Lynx. "Dreams do come true!" announced their flyers for the 6-horsepower putt-putt. The P-48 and P-49 models followed in 1948 and 1949 with the odd ad pitch, "It Looks Custom Built," meaning the unusual reinforcing crossbars welded in every direction were anything but streamlined.

Once the Korean War broke out, Powell was back to bombs. The company soon returned to the transportation arena in 1954, producing the ulti-

mate camper with a trunk designed for fishing rods, a pop-top camper, and wood bumpers by taking an old 1940s chassis off of a Plymouth. Taking mass-produced car accessories and putting them to new uses wasn't a stretch for Powell. After all, the A-V-8's ad pitch threatened that it used "replacement parts of a popular low-priced automobile." In 1967, Powell rediscovered its roots in scooterdom, however, with the Model L & M Challenger and Phantom mini-bikes with Tecumseh Briggs & Stratton engines.

Mustang Mini Motorcycles

Howard Forrest loved little things. Racing midget cars in the 1930s, he honed his skills in small-

Auto-Glide

THE HEART OF THE *Auto-Glide*
CUSHMAN HUSKY ENGINE

Here's the powerful automobile-type "CUSHMAN Husky air-cooled Engine, known for years as one of the very finest built. Cool in weight, but, Oh! Boy!—what an amazing performer it is! Complete with kick-starter, muffler, saint-type carburetor. Two sizes: 1 H. P. and 1½ H. P.

DISC CLUTCH
AUTO-TYPE "CUSHMAN" BUILT

The AUTO-GLIDE gets up speed quickly and smoothly from a standing start, because of its special Disc Clutch. Operates with a slight pressure of the left foot on the clutch lever. It has a spring-steel disc with double facing of faced velvet finish clutch material. Accurately machined. Easy to bring AUTO-GLIDE to a stop at intersections without killing the engine.

Over 120 Miles To The Gallon
More Than 30 Miles Per Hour

Operates Like An Auto .. Has Starter, Clutch, Throttle, Brake, Balloon Tires.

Here, at last, is Sensationally LOW-COST Transportation . . . and Delivery Service! Operates for actually ONE TENTH the cost of an auto! Only about ¼c per mile! Light weight . . . only 170 to 190 pounds, yet is built extra rugged throughout and powered with Cushman Engine.

Wheelbase, 49 inches. Built close to the ground, and is unusually easy to balance. It is the safest vehicle on the road—no center bar—just step off on either side. Seat only 28 inches from ground. Operates perfectly on dirt, gravel or paved road.

Comfortable and Convenient .. Fills the Gap Between the Bicycle and the Automobile.

AUTO-GLIDE has almost every feature you expect in a good automobile—and controls much like one. You start the Engine with a slight push on the handy kick-starter . . . Roll the machine with a little shove of your foot on the ground . . . throw in the smooth-as-velvet disc clutch—and You're Under Way! Convenient hand-throttle controls you speed up to 30 miles an hour, as the powerful Cushman Husky engine whisks you quickly to office, factory, school or a pleasure spin. Kari-Pac model is ideal for light deliveries.

The CUSHMAN MOTOR WORKS, LINCOLN, NEBR.

bore motors and peewee wheels. His newly purchased Salsbury Motor Glide lacked the power of his Indian big-twin, so he headed to the workshop.

He plucked a four-cylinder motor from one of his midget cars and managed to cram the whole thing into a Motor Glide frame. "The only things he didn't build on that engine were the spark plugs and the carburetor," Howard's son Jim Forrest later told *Classic Cycle Review*.

Unsatisfied with the chassis, Howard soon set to work designing his own frame and gearbox, and modifying a car radiator with a hand saw. Forrest's scooter-making prowess didn't go unnoticed while working as an engineer at Gladden Products. Owner John Gladden and engineer Chuck Gardner convinced him to go into the scooter business after World War II. Five different prototypes came to life in 1945 with two-stroke Villiers singles and suicide hand shifters. They were dubbed the "Mustang" after the P-51 Mustang fighter, and "Colt" because

larger motorcycles were supposedly in the works. Just as the Italians named their buzzing engine after a wasp, or *vespa* in Italian, Mustang's powerhouse engine carried the quaint name "Bumble Bee."

Never quite satisfied with the two-stroke Villiers, Howard Forrest was constantly hot rodding his bikes. He jammed a 350-cc BSA Gold Star engine into a Mustang Model 2 frame. He sawed a Triumph twin cylinder in half and shoved it into a Bumble Bee. He wedged a 597-cc English Ariel into a puny Mustang chassis with the whole shebang on petite 12-inch wheels. The result of all this putt-putt hot rodding was a motorcycle speed record of 100 miles per hour average at Rosamond Dry Lake in California.

Mustang was dynamite on the track with unbeatable handling for flat track racing. "Coming into a turn with a big motorcycle, you had to brake and set yourself up to slide through it," Mustang racer Walt Fulton recalled. "It was full throttle with the Mustang; you just turned it sideways and went."

Harley-Davidson was hard pressed to beat the mini Mustang. Even with Harley's hometown advantage Fulton beat out a new hog. "It was just me versus Carroll Resweber on a factory Harley-Davidson—a beautiful factory bike," Fulton remembers. "We went around and around trading the lead until he finally quit. He came in with blood running down his hands." The only way Triumph, Harley-Davidson, and Indian could beat Mustang was by convincing the American Motorcyclist Association to outlaw the Mustang's little wheels in Class C racing. Following his year with Mustang, Fulton joined the Harley race camp.

Undaunted, Mustang carved a niche for itself in producing these mini-motorcycles with every equine name in the book: Pony, Bronco, Stallion, and Thoroughbred. Still, in spite of attempts to diversify its market base, Mustang had to face the fact that consumers wanted either a car or a full-sized motorcycle. The year 1965 was a sad year for the scooter world since both Cushman and Mustang ceased their production lines.

Midwestern Motorscooters

Florence during the Renaissance, Paris in the 1920s, and the Midwest in the 1930s and 1940s were the places to be. Budding entrepreneurs began piecing together scooters with any available metal they could rustle up, then sell them to trusting family and friends.

Rock-Ola's bejeweled jukeboxes competed with live music beginning in 1935, just as the Chicago company pushed into the scooter market thinking it to be "America's Latest Craze!" The simulated-wicker siding in pressed metal doubled as an air duct to cool the 5/8-horsepower Johnson Iron Horse engine. David C. Rockola's brochures bragged that his delivery models could be used for, "Engravers, Electrotypers, Egg, butter, poultry and coffee routes, and Exterminators." Herb Singe archives

The Chicago-based Rock-Ola delved into the scooter world as a detour from the jukebox biz and "true weight" scales. The Rock-Ola economy scooter was the Tourist "equipped with the 3/4-horsepower motor"—making actual touring slightly out of the question. The Rock-Ola Deluxe model was "powered with the proven Johnson 1-horsepower engine," which it glorified as the "Iron Horse." Perhaps "iron goat" would have been more appropriate.

Further north in chilly Minneapolis, Minnesota, Comet Manufacturing tested the scooter waters by releasing a brochure featuring a Comet scooter that never went into production. Of the Comets that actually did cruise down the bumpy back roads of Minnesota, *Popular Science* wrote that the marvelous suspension was "frame and seat,"

avoiding the luxury of springs to protect the rider's gluteus maximus.

Midget Motors of Kearney, Nebraska, went one better, offering pure luxury on its 1938 Puddlejumper: "Any model available with parcel carriers, windshield for dust, rain, snow or winter operation, and even a powerful radio!" The scooter's streamlined styling and optional gas or electric engine was eons ahead of its time; one of the Puddlejumper models was "self-balancing" through the miracle of simply having three wheels.

Postwar, Gambles five-and-dime stores wanted to delve into the scooter battle against Montgomery Wards and Sears, Roebuck with a peewee putt-putt called the Doodlebug manufactured by Beam of Webster City, Iowa. The name was already

First weld a metal box to some tubes, drop in a 1/2-horsepower Lauson engine (skip the clutch), and borrow some of junior's 6-inch wagon wheels. Paint it blue and call it "keen." This 1945 four-cycle, two-speed wonder from Madison, Wisconsin, was nothing to be scoffed at, however. With an expanded 3-horsepower Lauson motor, the Keen lasted through the war with its parent company (then Strimple of Janesville) making tanks. Ad copy claimed not just transportation, but existential bliss since Power Cycles "actually cast monotony and everyday cares 'to the winds.'"

Postwar, Gambles Department stores wanted a piece of the scooter action that Sears and Wards were cashing in on. With a call to Beam Manufacturing in Webster City, Iowa, in 1946, the Doodlebug was born. Almost all other scooters made the Doodlebug the dwarf of puny scooters. Regardless, the 40,000 Doodlebugs on the road (and sidewalk) made its name synonymous with "scooter." Powered by a small 1 1/2-horsepower Briggs & Stratton or Clinton engine, the Doodlebug featured "7 Xtra features for Xtra riding joy!" including the special "Flexi-Matic clutch." Michael Dregni

synonymous for scooter throughout the United States, only this time Gambles copyrighted the word.

Nearly every motorcycle maker had taken a swipe at the scooter market after World War II. So in 1960, Harley-Davidson decided to throw its hat into the ring. While most scooters borrowed ideas from fighter planes, cafe racers, or sports cars, the Wisconsin wonder's Topper seemed to borrow its concept from a bass boat. With its fiberglass body and pull-start cord, it seemed like the perfect scooter for hauling in a Northern Pike. Despite being the little brother to world famous motorcycles, the Topper could never live up to Harley's rebel image, even with hipster Ed "Kookie".Byrnes from *77 Sunset Strip* pushing the model.

In his lengthy definitive history, *Harley-Davidson: The Milwaukee Marvel*, Harry Sucher allots the Topper exactly one sentence. Most books on the company regard the misunderstood puddle-jumper as a mistake better left to gather dust in the garage. Trying to get back to its old image, a Harley ad in 1987 showed a group of bikers and asked if you would sell an inferior product to these guys—unless of course it was a Topper.

Norman Siegal of Moto Scoot

"The Henry Ford of the scooter business."—*Time* 4/3/39

Norman "Abe" Siegal's legs ached and he was sick of dropping two bits to take the streetcar

The Harley Topper was a training bike for Hell's Angels but based less on a Shovelhead than a bass boat with its fiberglass body and pull-start engine. The 12-inch wheels were 2 inches bigger than on most scooters, and greater power came thanks to the 9.5-horsepower engine on the larger model. Unfortunately, Harley's timing was off since the Topper's debut in 1960 was at the tail end of the scooter craze. To spur lagging sales of its piglet, Harley signed on 77 Sunset Strip hero Ed "Kookie" Byrnes and plopped him on the two-tone Topper saying, "Kookie, lend me your TOPPER."

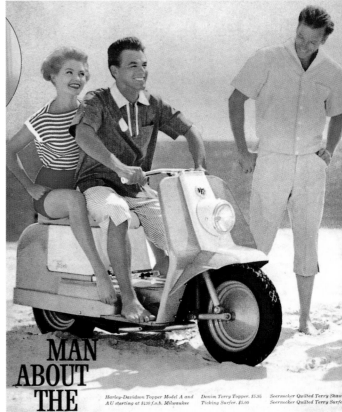

MAN ABOUT THE WORLD scoots about on nimble Topp

Harley-Davidson Topper Model A and AU starting at $430 f.o.b. Milwaukee — Denim Terry Topper, $5.95 Ticking Surfer, $5.60 — Seersucker Quilted Terry Shawl Seersucker Quilted Terry Surfe

Topper is thrifty, easy to handle and parks anywhere. *Scootaway* automatic transr smooth and effortless — places Topper above all other scooters. Economy? The great to 100 miles per gallon. Perfect balance, hefty brakes and large wheels produce comfort ride. Fashioned in fiberglass, stainless steel and aluminum — for the modern man in motion.

*T*OPPER BY HARLEY-DAVIDS

Harley-Davidson Motor Co., Milwaukee 1, Wisconsin

across Chicago in 1934. Siegal "got an engine from a gasoline-powered washing machine and he used two-wheels from my baby buggy," recalls his son Burt. "He rigged it up so he could hook it to the rear bumper of the car. People saw him riding it during the depths of the Depression and asked him to make one for them." Siegal's little invention made him a millionaire.

Siegal soon rented a Chicago storefront, promising to pay rent as soon as he sold his first batch of 10 scooters. Using old-fashioned American ingenuity, when he "ran out of metal [tubing for the frames], he broke a hole in the wall of his store, and pulled out a lead water pipe," recalls Burt Siegal. Thus the very first Moto Scoots were born. "When he got paid, he just replaced the pipe."

In 1936, when Norm was only 24 years old, he officially set up shop in part of a West Side Chicago factory and "by the end of the year he had sold 186 of them [scooters] at $109 apiece and had taken over the whole factory. In 1937 the output was 2,700, according to a 1939 *Time* article.

Surpassing retail sales of $500,000 in 1938, Moto Scoot moved to 8440 South Chicago Avenue. Siegal built a banked gravel race track running around the building so employees could let off steam by taking a couple of laps. (The winged Moto Scoot logo graced the marquee in the now rundown factory until 1996.) In a 1938 *Chicago Daily Times* article, Siegal summed up scooter riders saying that "he recommends it for the gent too indolent to walk to work and too anti-social to ride a street car."

Since Siegal had been on the county fair dirt-track circuit racing "Fronty-Fords" before he

pounded out his first puddle-jumper, he souped up a three-wheeled racing Moto Scoot and rented it to tourists at Navy Pier to let them feel the power of a two-stroke. He also worked on a rentable, two-seater "quarter-in-the-slot" scooter to zoom gawkers around the futuristic 1939 World's Fair.

Still gripped by racing fever from his "Fronty-Ford" days, Siegal built a half-sized racing Moto Scoot with a two-cycle Villiers engine and four-speed transmission that put the competition to

For a mere $111.50, this beautiful two-tone puddle-jumper could have been delivered to your doorstep in 1938. And for another 40 greenbacks, a side car could be tagged on, complete with fancy Moto-Scoot decals. "Make this your 'Declaration of Independence," announced early ads. Mead Cycle Co. of Chicago bought up a whole slew of Moto Scoots, slapped on some Mead Ranger stickers, and added these putt-putts to their line of "velocipedes" and "sidewalk-bikes." Delmar Baker

shame with its speed and maneuverability so much so that it was banned from flat track motorcycle races—or at least so Siegal claims. To celebrate his success in sales and racing, Siegal built a gold-plated Moto Scoot in 1941. But the tide was turning against him as hard times hit home. Steel became scarce as war production took precedence, and Moto Scoots weren't deemed essential for the war effort.

The war took its toll in 1941, when Siegal signed a chattel mortgage on his patents and machinery to make payroll. He ended up losing the Moto Scoot to "American Moto Scoot," which didn't begin scooter production again until 1945. Even

IWO JIMA AND THE PRICELESS SCOOTER CLUTCH

When Norm Siegal of Moto Scoot went off to the Far East with the Marines to serve his country, he had scooters on the brain. While bullets flew overhead, he lay in his trench and envisioned a new automatic clutch. He pieced together his brainstorm with spare parts he found, and carried the clutch with him everywhere, worried that someone would steal his idea before he could patent it. While storming the beaches of Iwo Jima, Siegal was manning a foxhole on the waterfront. To allow better mobility, he buried his clutch in the sand. After

he covered up the clutch, a couple of Japanese soldiers attacked from behind, killing his buddy and wounding Siegal.

He regained consciousness on an ambulance boat leaving Iwo Jima. Remembering his priceless clutch, he leapt to his feet, hopped on a skiff, and paddled back to shore. As he dug up the clutch, his commanding officer saw him and said, "If you can dig, you can fight," and handed him a gun. Wounded a second time, Siegal got off the island, but this time with his beloved clutch.

By the time Moto Scoot entered the 1940s, the welded tubular steel frame and optional Lauson, Clinton, or Stratton engines made this hump-backed "American Commuter" model a veritable speedster. "More Fun than Flying—And Far Cheaper," claimed early Moto Scoot ads for this "Magic Carpet of Bagdad!"

so, Siegal's vision of getting off the tram and onto a putt-putt was confirmed by *Popular Mechanics* in 1947: "[Scooters'] low cost of operation means it can be used for commuting to work daily at about the same expense as streetcar riding."

"Cushman": American Synonym for Scooter

Cushman Motor Works of Omaha, Nebraska, entered the scooter world by happenstance. No staff of highly trained engineers envisioned America's future being brought together coast-to-coast on Cushman two-wheelers. Originally begun in 1913, the Cushman family built the hearty Husky engine to power the likes of its Bob-A-Lawn mowers. The Depression hit hard, and in 1934 fellow Nebraska natives, the Ammons, bought out the Cushman plant. The Ammons envisioned this newly acquired factory as just an engine production line, but that would all change when a young neighbor boy zoomed

by in a pieced-together, rough-and-ready scooter.

The story began when aviator Colonel Roscoe Turner came to Nebraska with his daredevil air show in 1936. As a spokesman for Salsbury Motor Glides, Turner had his pilots ride to their planes on these barnstorming little putt-putts. "A neighborhood kid saw this scooter and decided that it would be fun to have one of his own. He found some angle iron and wheelbarrow wheels, and built himself a motorscooter. And he used a Cushman 'Husky' engine from a lawn mower to power it," according to Cushman President Robert Ammon in a 1995 interview.

When "Uncle Charlie" Ammon noticed the boy buying spare parts for his homemade gadabout, it sparked an idea and history was born. "The frame was made from 1 1/4-inch angle iron, but we soon learned that it wasn't enough. We then used 2-inch channel iron, which did the job," recalled Ammon. Of course this was the age before product liability laws, so if a scooter collapsed under the driver's hefty load, they just brought it back. "When I got the scooter stable enough that I could drive it without hands, I knew it was ready." This little prototype ran on a couple of 4x8-inch wheelbarrow tires and borrowed a Husky engine from a Bob-A-Lawn mower.

The Auto-Glide was an afterthought to Cushman, who was "in the business of building and selling engines. The idea of making a motorscooter was to build and sell more engines," according to Ammon. In fact, early Auto-Glides were crude machines with no suspension—just balloon tires and a padded seat. Even so, a 1937 Cushman letter

to potential buyers proclaimed the Auto-Glide "the very latest genuine AMERICAN THRILL." A brochure from the same year made the bizarre claim that driving an Auto-Glide was actually "NO COST AT ALL. Why, it's actually cheaper than walking." Apparently truth in advertising was optional.

The key to the scooter biz is to keep an eye on the competition and never let vanity get in the way of making enhancements. Ammon recalled how Cushman approached improvements: "I saw other scooters—Moto Scoot, Salsbury, Powell, and others. We would buy them to look them over to see what good features they had that we could incorporate.

"Own it! Maintain it! Operate it!" shouted ad copy from a 1949 Popular Mechanics regarding the coveted Cushman Model 52. This "family scooter" was constantly updated by Cushman. Simple but effective summed up these early Cushman scooters, and the ads didn't deny it, "You just turn the throttle on the right hand handlebar to go, and step on the brake pedal to stop." Michael Dregni

We also had lots of suggestions from dealers and employees within the company." Each year, the Auto-Glide was refined, at least until the dawn of World War II.

Since scooters were considered an economical form of civilian transportation during the war years, "we were making scooters when Ford couldn't get tires to make cars," remembered Ammon. The Cushman Model 53 was more than a way to burn rationed gas, however, and the 82nd and 101st Airborne decided that it was just the ticket to liberate Europe. Perhaps secret documents were leaked to the United States about Mussolini's Volugrafo paratrooper scooter, or confidential blueprints were shared with the British regarding the Royal Air Force's Corgi

Welbike; whatever the reason, the U.S. Army Air Force decided they needed a scooter secret weapon.

On April 29, 1943, Cushman responded to bids from the War department for an attack scooter. Cooper Motors of Los Angeles was one of the finalists on February 17, 1944, in Detroit, with the 5 horsepower Cooper War Combat Motor Scooter, according to secret "characteristic sheets" on various models tested. But when Army bureaucrats weren't satisfied with their visit to the Cooper factory, they turned around and gave the contract to Cushman. Cushman engineers got busy reinforcing the Airborne scooter to be dropped from the heavens deep into enemy territory. They pitched a rope over a tree branch, tied it to the Cushman, lugged it into the air,

"God is always on the side of the heaviest battalions," said Voltaire, and the Model 53 Airborne was a doozy, requiring two parachutes and extra metal reinforcing to brace its fall. Just as the Jeep and Humvee returned from active duty to showrooms, Cushman Scooters came marching home in civvies to the hearts of scooter collectors across the country as the Model 53A. Michael Dregni

Sears, Roebuck & Co. commissioned Cushman to build a line of scooters to sell in its department stores across the country. Usually Sears just tore off the Cushman logo replacing it with Allstate, but the 4-horsepower De Luxe model was a unique design available only through Sears. Underneath the smooth golf-cart like exterior lies essentially a Cushman Model 62 Pacemaker. Michael Dregni

and sent the scooter crashing to the earth. When the Model 53 had enough reinforcement to not fall apart, it was ready for the putt-putt Blitzkrieg.

Dutch scooter aficionado Kees Portanje recalls how the 1944 Cushman Model 53 liberated Holland. "We were hiding the carpet under the floorboards," said Portanje, talking about concealing all their possessions from the Germans. Then on September 18, 1944, "The Americans are here! I saw a Jeep, and the Americans came in." The

This rare 1960 Cushman Road King was half off-road dirt bike, half boxy modernism, but all "arm chair comfort." Earlier Road Kings weighed in at a hefty 310 pounds, and the 7.95-horsepower engine continually overheated. Luckily new air ducts in the side panels partially solved the problem.

Reading more like a religious tract than an advertisement, Cushman targeted teenagers, encouraging them to avoid an angst-ridden life of delinquency and convince Mom and Pop to splurge for a Pacemaker. A special section of the comic reads like a fun-filled driver's ed manual, and as always, there's no woebegone looks wrinkling the faces of these happy suburbanites. Jim Kilau archives

101st Airborne landed 8 kilometers outside of Eindhoven and soldiers came rolling into town on Cushman Airborne scooters.

When Cushman returned to civilian life after the war, the Auto-Glide name was dropped, opting for the now established "Cushman" title. The new line of 52, 52A, and 54 Cushmans was called "The Family Scooter." Updates included an automatic clutch on the 54 Model, and the long-awaited suspension to give that "F-L-O-A-T-I-N-G sensation"—at least until you hit a pothole.

Never content to rest on its laurels, Cushman brought Alfred Sloan of GM's idea of "planned obsolescence" to the scooter world with annual technological updates so fashionable folks would only want the latest model. "Most people think that obsolescence means the end. It means the beginning. People always live with obsolescent attitudes

Cushman was established in 1950 in Anderlues, Belgium, building bizarre versions of the American scooters complete with Husky engines, Cushman chassis, and imaginative (and never copied) styling. Even a three-wheeled delivery scoot was offered "for business, factories, Sunday drives, and sports."

Cushman hit its stride in the early 1950s with the Pacemaker and the early RoadKing scooters. Ammon remembered unabashedly, "We got some ideas from Vespa and Lambretta," just as Piaggio and Innocenti had originally gained inspiration from Cushman. As a result of these new models, the name "Cushman" became synonymous with "scooter" in the United States.

Always in search of a better putt-putt, Cushman disregarded Salsbury's "Five Commandments of Scootering" and bred a Harley Hog with a Doodlebug to produce the staple of the Cushman line: the Eagle. "Somebody in our sales department wanted a scooter that looked like a motorcycle with a gas tank between your legs. It turned out to be a hell of a good idea," said Ammon.

Spurred by postwar demand for a cheap "second car," the Eagle offered just the ticket. With rumors of a war in Korea circulating, *Business Week* pronounced, "War talk has brought a sellers' market in automobiles; it has also started a boom in the motorscooter field." During the first year of the Korean War, Cushman Motor Works expected to produce 10,000 scooters representing $3.5 million in sales.

Despite the Eagle's success, Cushman made dramatic improvements every couple of years. From the Super Eagle to the Silver Eagle, Cushman

and in obsolescent frames of mind and obsolescent technologies and homes," said cultural philosopher Marshall McLuhan. With heady concepts like this in mind, the Ammons brought out a dizzying array of models while other companies tended to just rehash the same old ideas.

Prewar ad pitches like "cheaper than shoe leather" and "sell more ice cream" were a thing of the past. An old 1939 ad boasted, "You can glide for 1/3 cent per mile!" now tripled to "1 cent a mile" in 1949. Inflation or gas guzzler? The quantity of oil burned was deleted from print ads. Perhaps consumers finally realized that the 1937 Cushman ad for "500 Miles on a Quart of Oil!" simply meant having to rebuild the engine every 1,000 miles.

Cushman pulled its weight in postwar reparations as part of the European Recovery Act. Belgian

WAR BREEDS NECESSITY

Although Lao Tzu's *The Art of War* never mentions motorscooters specifically, having the latest military gadget was not lost on this century's best military minds. Just as "In A.D. 1340, when firearms had not yet reached most of Europe, England's Earl of Derby and Earl of Salisbury happened to be present in Spain at the battle of Tarifa, where Arabs used cannons against the Spaniards. Impressed by what they saw, the earls introduced cannons to the English army, which adopted them enthusiastically and used them against French soldiers at the battle of Crécy six years later," according to Egon Larsen's *Ideas and Invention*.

The scooter followed the same trail, beginning in the 1910s when the Autoped was considered for active duty in World War I's trench warfare. Mustard gas mixed with two-stroke exhaust might well have changed the course of history.

Any successful poker-faced general knows that any scheme must be veiled with believable misinformation. We'll never know whether the leaked plans for the U.S. military scooter was a Trojan horse intended to convince the Axis to change its focus from V1 rockets and atomic experimentation to two-stroke paratrooping-putt-putts, whose noisy engines could easily be picked off by snipers. Nevertheless, busy military minds set to work hoisting scooters into trees and dropping them to earth in top-secret experiments. Italians dropped their minuscule Volugrafo Aeromoto fold-up paratrooper scooter from Piaggio planes; the United States employed the Cushman Model 53 Airborne Scooter; Britain pitched its Welbike from the sky; and previously top secret documents reveal that Russia was busy with a putt-putt project of its own to foil Hitler's blitzkrieg and perhaps the capitalist scum.

Very few scooters actually dropped from the heavens, however, since as Dwight D. Eisenhower said, "Do not needlessly endanger your lives until I give you the signal." Instead bureaucratic duties were delegated to "The scooters [that] were drafted into our war plants to deliver small parts between buildings," according to a 1947 *Popular Mechanics*. *Business Week* also wrote about scooters' purple-hearted service in 1946: "Sprawling war plants and the mobility-conscious armed services found a myriad of uses for the powered runabouts, which previously had been notable chiefly as a special headache to traffic safety planners."

updated its models with electric starters, better suspension, and larger engines. *Mechanix Illustrated* pronounced in 1956 that "Cushman scooters have all the soup the average American will ever need." *Popular Science* raved in 1957 of Cushman RoadKing's "Detroit Styling" because of its sporty two-tone, and pronounced that "thanks to an automatic clutch, the Cushman is the simplest to drive. Twist the throttle open, and you're off to a silk-smooth start every time." By 1957, 650 dealers across the United States were proudly displaying the latest models in their storefronts.

By the mid 1950s it seemed Cushman and the other scooter makers could do no wrong. Then

While the crewcut scooterists in Cushman ads may look like brainwashed astronauts, the pep of their M9 19.4-cubic inch engines proved they weren't so dim after all. "Swing into the saddle of this real man's machine . . . and GO! Feel the breakaway power of nine husky horses in the rugged new aluminum engine," bragged the brochures for this 1959 Series IV 765 Eagle.

came the backlash. Thousands of kids on scooters meant spiraling numbers of scooter deaths and injuries. Legislation was passed raising the minimum age of scooterists, but even so, teenagers were killed by scores. In Ohio alone, scooter mishaps resulted in 11 deaths and 412 injuries. An industry shill went on the offensive and declared that bicycles were responsible for twice as many deaths as these innocent putt-putts. Cushman put out comic books aimed at teenagers that were part advertising, part safety. *Business Week* praised Cushman's efforts in February 1959: "Cushman, while

"Learn a new definition of fun," urged a 1960 Super Eagle brochure, and what better way than with the telescopic front forks, 12-volt electrics, and the squared-off rear of the Super Eagle and its "streamlined" style. A buddy seat, roll bar, and chrome doodads have been added to this 1959 model, the year the Super Eagle debuted.

This 1957 150-cc Simplex tried to straddle the fence between the lucrative scooter market—in full boom by the late 1950s—and the macho motorcycle world. With a 48-inch wheelbase, whopping 4.00x20-inch wheels, but a step-through frame, "the Simplex is the first scooter to combine all the advantages of a Motorcycle and Scooter without any of the disadvantages of either type of vehicle." By the early 1960s, Simplex gave up its "motorcycle man's motorscooter" and delved into Sportsman mini-bikes, once again trying to appeal to two markets, "NOT TOO HEAVY—Not too LIGHT. The SPORTSMAN'S made JUST RIGHT for Man or Boy."

against legislation now pending, holds that dealers should make sure their customers have proper training. To this end, it has set up safety classes in several states."

Safety issues were not the final nail in Cushman's scooter coffin. Stiff competition from overseas that had recently entered the market, however, gave Cushman constant headaches. Rather than simply bowing out, Cushman decided to distribute Vespas itself beginning in 1961, attaching its own logo to the legshield as the "new" Cushman scooter. Many shocked dealers refused to roll over for the competition, and instead opted to sell Hondas. Ammon conceded that "The Hondas were just frankly better machines than the Cushman Eagles—and they were cheaper."

Prewar, Italian factories had been icons of technological progress that culminated with smokestacks puffing out soot. To most Italians this meant that they were indeed part of the industrialized world. But World War II had flattened Italian factories, erasing those once-tangible signs of progress.

The "Second Italian Renaissance" flourished in Italy following World War II as the age of mass mobilization hit even the smallest Italian hill town. In 1946, rubble was all that was left of the wartime factories, but the seed of knowledge to mass-produce machines had already been sown.

Barred from producing any war-related machinery, Innocenti and Piaggio rolled scooters out of the rebuilt factories to mobilize the masses. Ferdinando Innocenti and Enrico Piaggio looked to Henry Ford's assembly lines and surrounding

With the dawn of the Vespa Gran Sport at the end of 1954, Piaggio proved to the world that scooters were more than mere gadabout toys. Scooters were for racing. While Innocenti's early Lambretta was viewed as quicker—albeit less stylish—Piaggio put that theory to rest with the top-of-the-line GS. At least until 1957, when the Lambretta TV 175 took back the crown. Which of course prompted Piaggio to release the souped-up GS 160, the king of Vespas.
Mark Ulves

worker communities and turned their factories into born-again symbols of pride. Piaggio made the small town of Pontedera near Pisa into a working community, and citizens came from all over Italy looking for jobs. Undoubtedly the true sign of Italy's revitalization came when these factories rose from the ashes.

Piaggio Conquers the World

The Vespa's parent company, Piaggio, traces its roots to Rinaldo Piaggio's 1884 sawmill, which went on to build ships for the Italian navy. During World War I, Piaggio set up shop near Pisa, and became famous for its sturdy airplanes and the development of cabin pressurization in 1915. Piaggio even built Italy's only heavy bomber, the P108B, which killed Mussolini's son Bruno in a test flight crash. Building two- to four-engine planes during World War II, the Piaggio factory was the natural target to be flattened by B17 bombers.

Rising from the wreckage, Rinaldo Piaggio's sons Enrico and Armando kept the spirit alive by producing the Vespa. According to *Design* magazine in 1949, "The most important of all new Italian design phenomena is without doubt the Vespa."

The postwar saga began when designer Corradino d'Ascanio made a few sketches in February 1945 of a little scooter called MP6. The prototype

39

had a unique monocoque body and an attractive engine shield (which, unfortunately, induced a small overheating problem). Having originally been a helicopter designer, d'Ascanio easily worked out these early flaws, and his perfected scooter went on to mobilize the Italian masses. Fifty years later, d'Ascanio's Vespa made it into the Guggenheim Museum in New York as a tribute to Italian design.

Enrico Piaggio sang his company's praises in a 1956 *Time* interview: "Just like Henry Ford put the workers on wheels in America, we put automotive transport within the reach of people who never expected to travel that way." That same year, *Newsweek* reported that "1.5 million scooters were

While Piaggio's 1945 Paperino scooter was thought to be the dawn of the second Italian Renaissance, the idea actually stemmed from designer Vittorio Belmondo's SIMAT scooter and later the 1941 Velta VB model. A scaled-down version was licensed to Volugrafo, which dropped scooters from the skies as Italian lightning-brigade paratrooper putt-putts.

on the roads in Italy." Remote little villages that rarely saw outsiders now had buzzing Vespas braving the cobblestones of the town piazza. *American Mercury* reported in 1957 that "Wherever donkeys go, the Vespa goes, too."

But when Vespas were ready to cross the Atlantic, American magazines adopted a different attitude. *Business Week* in 1956 condescendingly called Vespas "little machines" driven carelessly thanks to "Italians' Latin enthusiasm." *The New Yorker* feared two-stroke fury zooming down Broadway and warned in 1956, "Motor scooters, the current scourge of sleep in Italian cities, have established a beachhead here . . ."

No matter what the Americans in their giant 1950s land barges thought, in Italy, the Piaggio brothers were heroes. When political turmoil threatened the Italian state in the 1960s, the major-

Piaggio designers Vittorio Casini and Renzo Spolti noticed Vittorio Belmondo's funny-looking SIMAT scooter and saw postwar Italian transport. Adding a legshield to Belmondo's basic design, Piaggio dubbed its creation the MP5 then nicknamed it the Paperino, or Donald Duck. The name came from Mussolini's language police who had insisted on changing American words to Italianisms: Mickey Mouse to Topolino, Goofy to Pippo, and Donald Duck to Paperino (little gosling). The scooter received a Sachs motor that was placed in a central position rather than off to the side as in later Piaggio scooters. Estimates of actual production numbers of the handmade Duck range from 10 to 100. Only two are known to still exist: One that is missing many parts at the Piaggio factory in Pontedera, and this complete Paperino discovered recently still running in a small Sicilian town.

ity Communist party was kept from power thanks to the CIA and the Vespa. Enrico Piaggio deemed it his patriotic duty to put his putt-putts within reach of the workers to lure them from Marxism. "The best way to fight Communism in this country is to give each worker a scooter, so he will have his own transportation, have something valuable of his own, and have a stake in the principle of private property," Piaggio told *Time* in 1952.

Owning a Vespa was an Italian's patriotic duty, and Italians responded in kind. "Roaring, darting scooters, outnumbering automobiles, dominate Rome's traffic. These toy-like vehicles have swept Italy since the war, almost replacing the motorcycle," according to a 1957 *National Geographic* article.

But greater popularity did not ensure greater safety of operation, and the media of the day was

Realizing the importance of scooters to the devastated Piaggio factory, Enrico Piaggio recruited his top aeronautic engineer Corradino d'Ascanio to design the MP6 prototype. D'Ascanio was a regular da Vinci, designing planes and helicopters, and now the 3.2-horsepower Vespa. "And this was how the Ugly Duckling (Paperino), as in Hans Christian Andersen's fable, became a swan, or rather a wasp (Vespa)," as La Vespa e Tutti i suoi Vespini put it. The scooter pictured was the 48th Vespa produced at which time any sort of rear suspension was only a dream.

The Vespa hit its stride in the 1950s with the 125-cc model that had enough get-up-and-go to carry a passenger on the optional pillion seat. Strict foreign regulations required the headlamp be raised to the handlebars.

quick to point out the scooter's failings. An article in the July 1962 *Atlantic Monthly* claimed:

> The makers of Vespas and Lambrettas, the two major Italian makes, use economy and maneuverability as their two main selling points. For many people, these are enough to make up for their relative lack of comfort . . . . Scooters are inherently unstable, like spinning tops. . . . On a scooter you lean over, and there you are, upside down in the ditch. You have to influence the scooter around a corner in a series of more or less controlled wobbles.

In spite of constant criticism regarding real or imagined safety problems, scooters were fairly easy to control for first-time riders. Besides, as a 1958 *New York Times* article pointed out, "if they fall over you're right there on the ground."

The two-stroke engine of the 125-cc Vespa was plenty to pull a speeding Vespista. Even plopping a passenger on the pillion seat wouldn't weigh down the scooter too much as long as the destination wasn't an Italian hill town. Add a sidecar to the equation—like this East Indian-built Cosy—and better hope for a nice incline, or a cool summer breeze from the rear to cool the engine and push the whole gang.

Innocenti

Innocenti set up its "factory communities" in the Lambrate quarter of Milan, equipped with swimming pools and tennis courts to keep the workers happy. The factory had become a Mecca of progress, or according to an Innocenti brochure, ". . . the modern new plant where a new LAMBRETTA comes off the assembly line every 60 seconds. Production techniques are the same space-age methods employed by famous jet aircraft and automobile manufacturers. Equipment, machinery

and procedures are determined by efficiency experts solely dedicated to producing perfect LAMBRETTA scooters."

Through technology and science, perfection became the ultimate goal. In an Innocenti promotional film, *We Carry On*, each scooter is like a *Sturmabteilung* storm trooper in that they are "machines which carry one name and one name only—a name which dominates the whole world." Each Lambretta clone was portrayed as a symbol of mechanical perfection. *We Carry On*, a requiem

In 1947, Piaggio released the Ape, or Bee, for small transport, or in this case as a maritime taxi/ricksha for open-air sightseeing and viewing picturesque sunsets on the island of Capri. With a few minutes effort, the canvas top would pop up to provide shelter from storms blowing in off the Tyrrhenian Sea. Piaggio also offered a larger five-wheeled Ape delivery mobile known as the Pentara. The jury's still out on whether the translation of Piaggio ads into pidgin English doomed sales abroad: "'Ape' Right for the job! The service rendered to the client in few minutes makes him satisfied, grateful and faithfull (sic) forever."

to the death of Ferdinando Innocenti, won the prize for best nonfiction film at the Cannes Film Festival in 1967. Piaggio had won the same award in 1961.

In his dense text on the Lambretta's image, Dick Hebdige quotes *We Carry On*. "[T]he production line

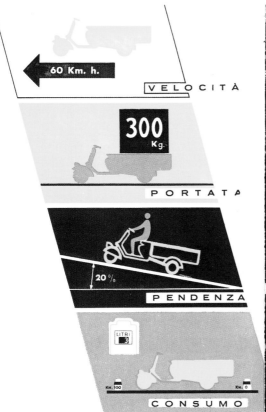

Hoffman's Die Königin (or queen) model ran off the German production line at the rate of 1,800 per month by 1953. When Hoffman tried to diversify into cars and mopeds in 1955, Piaggio was not pleased. Hoffman's license to produce Vespas was promptly transferred to the Messerschmitt factory until sales slumped and Piaggio decided to just export scooters directly from Italy in the 1960s.

46

Complete with a crèche in the background, a mid-1960s 125 Vespa maintains the original lines d'Ascanio envisioned in 1945.

is one mile long and one-third of a mile wide . . . .The factory is a hothouse in which the flowers are pieces of machinery. . . . the electromagnetic test bed is the altar of destruction on which will be sacrificed the body of a Lambretta. . . ." So as well as being a warrior, the Lambretta is also the messiah here to serve us.

To evangelize the world, Innocenti set up factories in Argentina, Brazil, Colombia, Congo, India, Indonesia, Pakistan, Spain, Sri Lanka, Taiwan, and Turkey. By the 1970s, scooter sales had plummeted in Europe and the United States, but the Third World kept the spirit alive.

Alas, the Innocenti factory in Lambrate today lies vacant. After having switched to a doomed enterprise in mini cars, the city of Milan planned to turn the enormous building into a shopping mall. This sacrilege was thwarted, but now the only residents are pigeons.

The Scooter Gets Religion

All this talk of the scooter as savior didn't seem to bother the Holy See, however, as the millionth Vespa was officially blessed by the Vatican on an altar. The Church saw the scooter as a means for the masses to get to Mass on time. Much to the Vatican's delight *Time* reported in 1956: "More people were baptized in 1955; more went to Communion this Easter than ever in history. One reason: motor scooters." The article went on to say:

> Priests in Italy, according to a Vatican report, currently own 30,850 motorscooters, and in terms of sacraments and good works, the average priest's efficiency has climbed to about 3,000 percent over that of his road-trudging nineteenth century predecessor. Another straw in this high wind is the decline of the more introverted Benedictines and foot-slogging Franciscans in favor of the fast-moving Jesuits,

whose high-octane practicality thrives on the motor-scooter age. Pope Pius XII has been a longtime friend of automation; last fall he called for "greater and greater speed to the glory of God."

Life Magazine rebutted this slam of Franciscans, however, in 1957 with a photo of a Capucin "Brother Henry" zooming down Baltic Street in Brooklyn on his Vespa with a sidecar pulling a roller skater.

The Vatican continues to give thanks to the wonderful Vespa to this day. Pope John Paul II has twice had an audience with the president of the Fédération Internationale des Vespa Clubs, Christa

Both the 90 Super Sprint and the 50 Super Sprint (pictured) were Piaggio's challenge to the diminutive motorcycle market aimed at teens looking for speed. When Piaggio gave birth to the Vespa 50 in 1962, the "Vespino" instantly became the best-selling scooter in its lineup. The souped-up Super Sprint, like this Geneva-made SS50, with narrow handlebars, front legshield, the sporty extra gas tank, and spare tire between the legs made even the quietest Italian piazza a mini Monza for teenagers.

Solbach, and has given his papal blessing to scooterists the world over.

"A New Race of Girls"

Scooters were designed with women in mind. *Popular Mechanics* wrote in 1947, "As the family's second 'car,' the scooter makes shopping a pleasure for the housewife."

Scooters had served to emancipate women even before Amelia Earhart was pictured aboard a Motoped. Female suffragists in the 1910s zipped down U.S. sidewalks on their dangerous little Autopeds, just as their British counterparts stepped on the running board of ABC Skootamotas in the 1910s.

But it took unabashed, Vespa-mounted Italian divas like Gina Lollobrigida and Anna Magnani to add spice to the otherwise staid postwar scooter. A 1954 *Picture Post* article wrote about "'A New Race of Girls,' untamed, unmanicured, proud, passionate, bitter Italian beauties [on their] clean, sporting Vespas . . . ."

Italian scooter designers had always considered women in their designs. In fact, when Piaggio designer Corradino d'Ascanio assembled the first Vespa, the gas tank was removed from its position between the rider's legs so dresses could be easily worn. Citing this improvement, *The New York Times* magazine wrote that, "Another visible difference [from motorcycles] is that scooters do not have a center bar for the driver to straddle. This makes for more girl riders and less Ghent-to-Aix forward lean." Since many gussied-up Italian women insisted on high heels, the motorcycle foot shifter was left by the wayside, replaced by a hand shifter to simplify gear changes.

As scooter designs meshed with women's clothes, so fashion changed to maximize riding ease. "The narrowing of the new-look skirt was dictated in order to prevent it getting tangled up with the wheels. The slipper shoe was created for footplate comfort. The turtleneck sweater and neckerchief were designed against draughts on the neck," according to a *Picture Post* article of 1950. Trousers were soon the rage, since skirts inevitably blew

When the D appeared at the end of 1951, the fate of the "uncovered" Lambrettas had already been sealed by the previous year's "sheathed" LC (L for Lusso, or Luxury). Many loyal Lambrettisti scoffed at Innocenti's attempt to copy the Vespa's full covering of the engine, but the Italian people loved the style and the more powerful Innocenti engine. When Italian scooter aficionados look back on Innocenti's zenith, inevitably they get teary eyed for uncovered models like this D (even though it's missing its horn). Innocenti straddled the fence trying to please both sides, and continued to manufacture the open style scooters until 1956 with models A through F.

The LD kept the basic styling of the LC with minor modifications, and larger production numbers, allowing export into the United States. Popular Science wrote about the LD, "Like other two-stroke power plants, it's fond of revs, and the constant-mesh three-speed transmission lets you take full advantage of this at all times." Michael Dregni

back, and headkerchiefs kept the new moptop hair-dos in place. Sunglasses became a cool necessity, ensuring hipness and clear vision. Still, not all in scooterdom were pleased with fashion trends, Innocenti's prudish newsletter *Lambretta Notizario* lamenting that "one is all too-frequently tormented by the sight of badly trousered women on motor scooters."

In spite of the obvious pains taken by scooter designers to attract and accommodate female riders, magazine articles inevitably placed her on the pillion seat—and usually in a dangerous sidesaddle position to boot. A 1957 *Popular Mechanics* article even endorsed this hazard stating, "Two persons can ride one at the same time, but a woman wearing a skirt (particularly if it is a straight one) must ride sidesaddle if she is the passenger." In that same year, a Vespa accessory catalog even featured an uncomfortable Poltrovespa sidesaddle seat.

A 1957 article in *National Geographic* on Italy featured a woman on a scooter, but again delegated her to the back seat. "Women ride, too. When papa drives, mamma sits sidesaddle on the box seat, often with a baby in her lap. Youngsters stand

The scooterization of the United States in the 1950s was complete with the introduction of the LD and the resulting hubbub in the press for the economical and stylish putt-putt. Available for a mere $379.50 (or $329.50 for the stripped-down D model) when it entered at Ellis Island for Barkas & Shalit distribution in New York, the LD soon hit showrooms across the country. Popular Mechanics raved in 1957 about its 100 miles per gallon "that's economical traveling in any man's language."
Roberto Donati archives

Lambretta

INNOCENTI

Jayne Mansfield

While Twiggy may have been the appropriate model to pose on the new Slim Style Li Lambrettas, her fee was an outrageous 80 quid an hour. Innocenti, nevertheless, scored when jumpsuited Jayne Mansfield agreed to pose on the new modded-out, two-tone Lambrettas. David Gaylin/Motor Cycle Days

Ms. Mansfield showed the world that blondes prefer Lambrettas, and Innocenti was forever in her debt. In commemoration, a one-of-a-kind gilded Lambretta was prepared with even the smallest accessory gold-plated. This slimline now resides at Vittorio Tessera's Lambretta Museum outside of Milan.

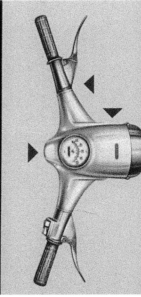

TOP

With dissecting schematics and bloodlike colors, this anatomical view of Lambretta innards shows the pathways of ingested petrol through the 21-millimeter Dell'Orto carb. The bulbous bodywork followed the automotive styling of the day. The TV was simply one of the fastest, most affordable scooters on the road, and it became the heart-throb of many a mod headed for the Isle of Man scooter races. Innocenti soon responded to the young Brit lust for speed and style and offered two-tone TV 200s based on Eddy Grimstead's paint jobs from Barking Road in London. Collezione Vittorio Tessera

While perhaps not as collectable as the larger cc scooters, the Cento is nevertheless a testament to the endurance of Inno-centi engines. Production may have stopped in the 1970s, but the little puddle-jumpers can still be seen in piazzas around Italy, like this one spotted near the Forum in Rome. The mini Lambrettas were popular because Italian law allowed teenagers to cruise around town without a license.

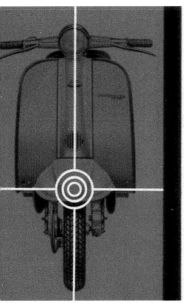
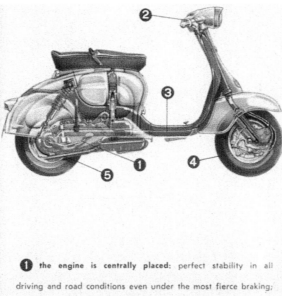
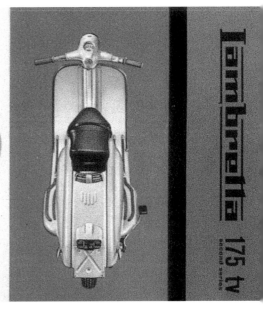

① the engine is centrally placed: perfect stability in all driving and road conditions even under the most fierce braking;

Located outside of Milan, Iso's reputation was cemented when its refrigerators made the iceman obsolete. In 1948, Iso assembled its first scooter, the 65-cc powered Furetto. Iso owner Renzo Rivolta was so disgusted by the ugly little scooter that he allegedly dug a hole and threw it 6 feet under to preserve his reputation. In 1950, Iso produced a 125-cc gem (pictured) that sold throughout Italy at 2,500 dealers, making Iso a threat to Piaggio and Innocenti. This second series stayed in production until 1956, when the Iso Diva, a.k.a. Milano, took the helm. Iso diversified with the Isetta mini car, which was later licensed to BMW. Then in the 1960s, Iso turned its back on the scooters that made it great to produce gran turismo sports cars.

between seat and handlebars."

According to cultural historian Dick Hebdige, male British Mods had the same "women on the back" attitude and often belittled their girlfriends as mere "pillion fodder." In the United States, attitudes portrayed in the monthly *American Mercury* in 1957 weren't much better, ". . . she riding sidesaddle prettily and revealingly and he, heading deliberately for every bump to jounce her into holding him tighter . . ."

While the media put women on the pillion, scooter companies were more than happy to have them in the driver's seat, since it meant a whole new market. Innocenti ads featured women on scooters, and while the annual Piaggio calendars consisted of cheesecake snapshots, at least the women were *riding* the Vespas.

Innocenti actually turned the tables on the backseat rider in a 1954 advertising film *Travel Far, Travel Wide*, echoing Amelia Earhart's famous photo on a Motoped. In the movie, a shiny new Vespa waits on an airport runway. As a stewardess gets off the plane and on to her putt-putt, the voice-over announces, "The air hostess can become the pilot herself—and there's plenty of room on that pillion for a friend!" The male pilot then hops on the pillion and women's emancipation is complete.

A small factory in the picturesque town of Reggio Emilia put together a doozy of a scooter in the early 1950s, long before giants Piaggio and Innocenti had perfected their styling. SIM (Società Italiana Motorscooter) borrowed a Puch two-cylinder 125-cc engine worthy of 85 kilometers per hour and added swan wing chrome on the side panels and a hood ornament. In spite of the attention to detail, SIM only produced a few of the Moretti scooters.

The Ducati scooter was the Cadillac of its day, with a powerful 7.5-horsepower, 175-cc engine, 12-volt electrics, an electric starter, and automatic transmission. All this from 1952 to 1954 when the competition was busy producing primped mopeds, worrying more about paint schemes than speed. The noted designer Ghia put the cherry on top when he envisioned a fabulous two-tone paint job that would later be copied by mods and "with-it" scooter makers. The only drawback was that the Cruiser was too fast, easily surpassing speed limits, which forced Ducati to detune the scooter to a maximum of 80 kilometers per hour. Vittorio Tessera

Promoting stereotypes, Mechanix Illustrated wrote in 1956, "The Italian-made Rumi is up to German standards in respect to power, speed and workmanship but sells for an attractive Italian price—$395." This 1955 two-cylinder Rumi Formichino, or little ant, was truly a masterpiece commissioned to the artist Donnino Rumi, son of Rumi's founder. While other scooters covered the grimy engine, the Formichino proudly displayed the 125-cc motor as an integral part of the frame. Note the cast-aluminum chassis.

57

Italy may have set the standard for scooters, but each European country added its own panache to the original formula. German putt-putts were solid, reliable, and powerful; French designs offered bizarre styling cues in the spirit of that quintessential example of Franco design, Renault's 2CV; and British scoots were fast, stylish, and, of course, unreliable.

Deutschland's Motorrollers

While one of the first motorcycles was invented by Gottlieb Daimler of Kannstatt, Germany, in 1885, scooter production had to be imported. Apart from some turn-of-the-century experiments, putt-putts reached Deutschland via Italy and construction began just four years after the end of World War II.

The first German company to roll Italian scooters off its production line was Hoffmann Werken near Düsseldorf in Lindorf. *Die Königin* Vespa pro-

While the Maico Mobil ranks as the most beautiful and bizarre scooter, its nasty nickname, the "Dustbin" brought it down a notch. This beautifully restored 175-cc second series model came into the world in 1956, at which time Maico had just begun making the more sporty (and sleek) Maicoletta scooter. The Maico's legendary "Auto auf 2 Rädern," or car on two wheels, gave way to the scooter on two wheels. Vittorio Tessera

duction then transferred to former Luftwaffe supplier Messerschmitt, near Augsburg, in 1955. When scooter sales slumped in 1963, however, Piaggio took away licensing and returned production to Pontedera in Tuscany.

Innocenti selected former Wehrmacht tank supplier NSU (Neckarsulm Sewing Machine Union) to create German Lambrettas. Volkswagen molded the metal for the putt-putts, and Innocenti produced the engines. In 1956, Lambretta licensing was halted in Germany, and the scooters were imported from Milan. Despite the setback, NSU found new inspiration. The Italian peculiarities inherent in Lambrettas had frustrated German engineers, but they were soon mended by good old Teutonic engineering. Logical improvements like a real fuel gauge were lauded by *Mechanix Illustrated* in 1956. NSU ad copy went even further: "Above all, the NSU-PRIMA is recognized by most people as the most beautiful motor scooter." Vespa may have been the Volkswagen Beetle of scooters, but NSU's Prima was definitely the 1957 Chevy, with bulbous bodywork, acres of chrome, and air intakes everywhere. The NSU Prima was so snazzy even Bob Barker asked his TV contestants on *The Price is Right* to debate its market value. And the answer is? $555.

Soon scooters were popping off German production lines from makers like Adler, DKW Auto

Mr. Smith riding to his work

will save a lot of time in the morning, for his ADLER-JUNIOR will carry him swiftly and punctually to his distination, while some less enlightened fellow citizens are getting crushed in overcrowded trains, trams or buses.

Having an extra forty winks in the morning, being home earlier in the evening, those are comforts all owners of an ADLER-JUNIOR soon learn to appreciate . . . . .

Here's what Mr. Smith likes best about the ADLER-JUNIOR: -

*

The long-stretched double swinging-arm running gear and the large 14" wheels which ensure a truly ideal roadholding;

*

The power and economy of the proven ADLER engine. Its quick starting, easy hill climbing and steady perseverance on the motor highway can be taken for granted and need hardly be mentioned at all;

*
The powerful - brakes responding to a slight touch as well as to a split-second emergency action. The reliable brakes and superior roadholding impart a feeling of absolute safety in any situation

ADLER*) will lend you wings!
*)'Adler' is the German word for 'Eagle'

*
Simple and comfortable:
the heel-and-toe foot change

Adler mobilized Germany with bicycles beginning in 1898, and moved into the realm of scooters by 1955 with the 98 cc Junior and the 125 cc Junior Luxus. "Live joyfully with wings—drive an Adler," proclaimed a 1955 pidgin English ad. The Adler Junior was one of the few German scooters to be imported into the American market.

Union (later MZ), Faka, Goggo, and Simson. Simson advertising copy read, ". . . be independent of the means of communication of the large city, save time and make distances become relatively little, SIMSON Moped or the SIMSON Small Size Scooter are the ideal vehicle. . . ." Even the American handyman journal *Mechanix Illustrated* extolled the virtues of German scooters in 1956, "With top speeds running up to 70 mph-plus and powered by big two-stroke mills, the Jerry jobs are loaded for bear—and the buyer had better be loaded with dough, by scooter-buying standards."

Scooterists opting for Progress scooters were lured to earthly wanderlust by the model name *Strolch*, or *vagabond* in German. With an unusual pivoting headlamp on the front apron, the Progress—with optional engines from 150 cc to 200 cc—was backed by ads of romantic getaways to the beach and mountains.

Progress licensed its scooters to a British firm, but the names were changed to the more English-sounding "Briton," "Anglian," and "Brittania." The German TWN Triumph, based in Nürnberg, built the Contessa scooter based on its "whispering

Erhard Doppelt added a single-cylinder engine and some attractive British racing green siding to a German bicycle and conceived the Meister Roller. Perhaps more moped than scooter, the 1955 Meister had a slight 47-cc engine pushing its spoked wheels to a less-than-blistering 40 kilometers per hour, barely enough to pass up its bicycles.

The Triumph story began in Coventry, England, when a pair of Germans formed a bicycle company in 1897, then moved into motorcycles in 1903. They opened a factory in Nürnberg that split from the English Triumph in 1929 to become TWN (the British portion was TEC Triumph). While TEC dragged its feet in making the Tigress scooter with BSA, TWN built the Tessy and the beautiful Contessa, pictured. Hans Kruger archives

Just like Adler, Dürkopp began as a pedal pusher with bicycles in 1867, then in 1954 upgraded to scooters. Paying homage to the goddess of forests, Dürkopp dubbed its 9.5-horsepower puddle-jumper the Diana. The Tourist Superb and the pictured Sport model both had a fan-cooled 194-cc engine with four speeds, but only the Sport's higher compression pushed its top speed to 100 kilometers per hour with 12 horsepower.

mit der Zeit gehen!

Goggo ... fahren

Chronicling the history of the wheel from antique cars to bicycles, this stylish young fräulein tells us to "Go with the times! Drive . . . Goggo." The luxury 125-cc or 150-cc scooter with a porky fender, however, was a knockoff of the Goggo Mobil mini-car with suicide doors made by Hans Glas GMBH. Hans Kruger archives

perhaps be more appropriate because her pretty little fingers will not be enough for the many advantages." How true it was! With an optional electric starter, two luggage carriers, and teardrop, two-tone styling, the Tessy was every German's dream motorroller.

Dürkopp sought the female market with 175-cc and 200-cc two-wheelers. By allowing Miss Germany of 1954 to "win" a Diana, Dürkopp proved its scooters to be the ultimate steed for the modern

Once free of German shackles, the Bernardet Frères set to work after the war producing some of the most chic putt-putts on which to be seen in front of the neighborhood bistro. The long wheelbase offered stability rarely seen on imports, and the split-single 250-cc Violet engine on most Bernardets made them win any drag race with a Vespa. In the mid-1950s, French fascination with cowboys hit the Salon de Paris and a Texan version of a Bernardet—complete with saddle horn on the pillion pad, leather fringe hanging from the handlebars, and simulated rhinestone saddlebags—was produced. Unfortunately for the rest of the world, Bernardets were seldom seen outside France.

motorcycle," and the Tessy in 1956. Ad copy read, "The young lady isn't actually using her fingers to count the number of her admirers, but the advantages of the TESSY. An adding-machine would

This 1957 Zündapp Bella Model 203, was originally purchased from a Harley-Davidson dealership in Maine before the Milwaukee Miracle took a turn into scooters themselves. Perhaps if Harley had learned from Zündapp how solid and speedy a scooter could be, America would be crawling with Harley Toppers.

fräulein. Dürkopp's entry into the scooter realm surpassed its struggling motorcycles sales, but only lasted until 1960, at which time it returned to its roots, sewing machines.

Heinkel focused less on attracting women scooterists and more on building a solid touring scoot. In 1922, Ernst Heinkel began building war materiel, especially airplane parts, for the fatherland. During World War II, Heinkel gave the Allies reason to quiver—its huge bombers caused blackouts across England. Postwar, the rubble that was once a factory was reduced to making scooters. But from difficult circumstances rose the four-stroke 1953 Heinkel Tourist 101. While Germany's world

domination may have been snuffed, Heinkel scooters succeeded in exporting German tourists to all parts of the globe during its 12-year reign.

Soon scooters were circling the globe as a status symbol for both the nouveau riche and old money. Royalty such as his majesty Lord Montagu proudly rode his 1950 Lambretta B; his grandeur Prince Rainier and Princess Grace hopped on a 1959 Lambretta Li 150 Series 1. But it was only when the gigantic high-class German 197-cc Maico Mobil hit the market that the illustrious King Hussein of Jordan could be satisfied.

Before the war, Maisch and Co., the manufacturer of the Maico Mobil, resided in "a peaceful section of the South German countryside, in which both the main works at Pfäffingen and the MAICO Engine Works at Herrenberg are situated," according to 1955 Maico information bulletin. Postwar, Pfäffingen was in the French section of Germany, and the factory was reduced to making toys. Then in 1951 the mammoth Maico Mobil was introduced, a scooter that "will prove to be the true touring machine of the future," according to

Piaggio licensed the German Hoffmann-werken to build the Die Königin "Queen" scooter, but this 1950 Vespa ad was an obvious rip-off of an earlier Lambretta ad with a boy and his dog trying to keep up. Roberto Donati archives

Maico adman H. W. Boensch. The most outlandish scooter ever to hit the autobahn, it made believable all those scooter brochure references to the "car on two wheels." Thanks to huge leg

With only seven remaining in existence of the 1,200 made, the top-of-the-line Einspurauto (one-track car) has become one of the most collectable putt-putts to scooter museums across Europe. With a French design by Monsieur Lepoix and German production in aluminum, the Bastert unfortunately only lasted from 1952 until 1956. Its 13-inch wheels and relatively low seat made for a low center of gravity and smooth ride powered by either a 174-cc or 197-cc engine.

shields and a powerful 175-cc or 200-cc engine, "this was to be in no sense a copy of an existing machine, but rather a completely new vehicle suited to German weather conditions."

Although the Mobil's successor had to live in the enormous (literally) shadow of the Dustbin, the Maicoletta was one of the fastest, most solid scooters ever built. The German design team of Pohl and Tetzlaff worked by candlelight fearing that corporate spies would steal their design, finally unveiling the 175-cc and 250-cc Maicoletta in 1955. It was soon equipped with a tremendous 275-cc engine, jamming 14 horsepower into the little chassis and

making it the most powerful putt-putt in German scooter history.

While Zündapp of Nürnberg was famous for its wartime motorcycles, the damaged factory produced potato mashers postwar. In 1952, Zündapp sneaked a 125-cc Parilla Levriere scooter back from Italy, and the following year the 150-cc Bella was born. The Bella was soon updated with a larger 200-cc engine, and by 1959 the R204 Bella was judged "amongst the best scooters on the market" by *Motor Cycling* magazine.

After a long, proud scooter history, Zündapp elected to sell out all its remaining merchandise to the

In keeping with the liberal mentality that made France great, SICRAF (Société Industrielle de Construction et de Recherches Automobiles de France) borrowed liberally from early Lambretta design, masking the imitation with a slightly darker paint job. This stylish S149 model with a peppy 125-cc Ydral motor was all the rage to cruise through the Arc de Triomphe on a moonlit night. Paul Vallée lost its touch, however, when it veered into the abyss of three-wheeled vehicles with a doozy called "The Singing Cleric." François-Marie Dumas archives

People's Republic of China in 1985. About 1,500 Chinese comrades traveled overland in a freight train all the way to Munich. For two weeks they loaded up all the machinery and remaining stock, sleeping in the boxcars at night to save money, and headed back to Asia to set up shop.

France

The first scooter to be seen in force in France was the Italian Vespa, which soon was manufactured under contract by Ateliers de Construction de Motocycles et d'Accessoires (ACMA). French law required that the headlamp be relocated from the front fender to the handlebars, and that bicycle pedals be placed on the small 50-cc Vespinos (they were insultingly considered mopeds). ACMA also shrunk the large tires on the GS from 10 inches to 9 inches in 1958. ACMA's most extraordinary modification was the fitting of a 75 millimeter cannon to create an attack Vespa for mobile troops.

Monsieur Ham debuted a Motobécane/Motoconfort scooter at the Salon de Paris in 1951 equipped with a four-stroke, 5-horsepower engine and style that could only come from Parisian showrooms. Lovingly dubbed the "Mobyscoot," the SC added reverse hand levers and sleek but rotund lines to Ham's original design. François-Marie Dumas archives

These two beautiful Peugeot scooters broadened this French car manufacturer's base into the world of two-strokes while other auto makers were stuck in the four-wheel rut. The red Peugeot S55 dates from 1955, two years after its smashing debut in 1953. The other Peugeot S57 from 1958 showed the world that the front fender of the scooter could be more than wasted space and placed a handy glove box there. François-Marie Dumas archives

Innocenti wasn't about to let Piaggio steal the show, however, so it signed on Société Industrielle de Troyes to pump out its putt-putts in 1952. Another French company, Paul Vallée had already started making Lambretta clones, so Innocenti's scooters seemed more like a copy rather than the original.

Bernardet scooters, on the other hand, showed the world that French style was still original. Three Bernardet brothers teamed up after France's liberation to design outlandish two-tone styling and never-copied bodywork, which gave the illusion of speed even when standing still. The long wheelbase offered a steady ride in all models. The initial 128-cc Ydral engine was updated in 1949 to a hefty 250-cc split-single Violet engine featuring an unusual left-side kick start. Unfortunately for scooter aficionados everywhere, Bernardets never crossed the Rhine, English Channel, or Pyrenees so the rest of the world could gawk at pure speed.

While most scooter manufacturers were looking for a quick buck in what they thought was a scooter gold mine, Peugeot entered the scooter world for keeps. To prove the longevity of its two-strokes, two French air force quarter marshalls braved a ride from Saigon to Paris in 1956, arriving down the Champs Elysées to almost as much fanfare as Lindbergh's transatlantic flight from New York. That same year, Peugeot bulked up the tires to 10 inches and increased horsepower. Peugeot took a hiatus from the scooter world in the 1960s

Built by Brockhouse Engineering and originally designed to serve the RAF as the Excelsior Welbike, this paratrooping putt-putt dropped from the sky striking fear into the hearts of the Luftwaffe. Postwar, its moniker was softened to that of the royal canines, the Corgi. Indian motorcycles even imported the odd little scooter, calling it the Papoose.

The Spanish Derbi was an acronym for Derivados de Bicicletus. Its 1953 model name, "Masculino," reeked of bravado even though the poky 98-cc or 125-cc engine hardly flexed any macho brawn.

and 1970s, but returned in force in the 1980s with the plastic Metropolis, Fox, and Rapido scooters. To this day the French firm pumps out plastic scoots appealing to Europeans who can't find the spare change to upgrade to the new Vespa.

Britain

"These are to certify that by direction of His Royal Highness The Prince Philip, Duke of Edinburgh, I have appointed Douglas (Kingswood) Ltd. into the place and quality of Suppliers of Vespa

The Defiant stood by its name and refused to have a nose job. DKR of Wolverhampton, England, came to the scooter world with the Dove scooter in 1957, followed by the ambitious sounding 148-cc Pegasus and 197-cc Defiant the next year. The line kept speeding up with a 249-cc Manx scooter in 1959. Didier Ganneau

Attempting to cash in on the English lust for anything Italian, in 1952 Cyclemaster (Britax) put into production Vicenzo Piatti's mini hovercraft in two models: a two-speed 98 cc and a three-speed 125 cc. Les Anciens Establissements D'Ieteren of Belgium also took up the design boasting, "Total Stability either with or without a passenger." Wow!

Scooters to His Royal Highness," heralded a 1967 Royal Warrant.

The Vespa invasion into Britain had actually begun about two decades before His Royal Highness confirmed his scooter preferences when Claude McCormack, head of the Douglas motorcycle firm, went for an Italian holiday in the sun in 1948. While other tourists cursed those "dang" scooters ruining their snapshots, McCormack had an epiphany. By 1949, Douglas had begun importing Vespas into Britannia adding a chrome "Douglas" above the Vespa logo on the legshield. By 1951, Piaggio had licensed Douglas to build British

Vespas and the 125-cc 2L2 Douglas Vespa hit the streets of London in March of that year. Soon London vacationers didn't need to head south to hear two-stroke buzzing night and day.

J. Symonds in a mid-1950s issue of *Design* magazine mourned the lack of British scooters on the market and lamented the rise of imports in an article entitled, "Where are the British Scooters?" English motorcycle manufacturers worried about the rise of scootering. According to what seems like an exaggerated account by historian Dick Hebdige, "the trend had become pronounced: at the 1955 Earl's Court Motor Cycle Show, three motorcycles were on display competing against 50 new scooters." The Empire responded, and soon scooter names like Bond, Excelsior Monarch, and Piatti were buzzing around England. Even bicycle legend Raleigh teamed up with Bianchi to build Roma scooters under license.

Bowing to the fact that the Rockers had lost the battle for media attention to the Mods, the two café racer moguls, BSA and Triumph teamed up in 1959 to produce one of the slickest, fastest scooters ever to drive on the left side of the road, the Tigress (Triumph)/Sunbeam (BSA). Even the

One of the coolest scooters ever to hit pavement, the Tigress was a latecomer to the putt-putt arena as motorcycle giants Triumph and BSA finally bowed to scooter mania and teamed up to produce a 250-cc gem in 1960. Alas, this luxury scoot with a whopping twin cylinder, four-stroke engine was too late on the scene. The other nail in the BSA Sunbeam/Triumph Tigress coffin was its distribution primarily through motorcycle dealers, an inferno any self-respecting Mod would avoid like the plague.

new Vespa of 1995 surely stole design cues from these scooters' teardrop go-fast lines. A BSA Sunbeam ad for the 250-cc twin declared, "Cruise at highway speeds—enjoy smooth power flow. . . . Stop with powerful new design brakes [sic]." BSA/Triumph works racers ran one of the scooters for 10 hours straight traveling a total of 510 miles with a top speed between 65–70 miles per hour. With the two biggest motorcycle makers in England behind the Tigress/Sunbeam, designer Edward Turner boasted that "we can make as many machines as the public wants . . . factories have the capacity for at least 50,000 scooters a year." Turner's dream wasn't to be, since by 1965 the fickle English public was instead opting for Morris Mini Minors.

While Triumph had succeeded in establishing a loyal niche for the British buyer who wanted a domestic machine, the market couldn't justify continued scooter production. Triumph's last model, the T10—a glorified Tina scooter—sang its swan song in 1970.

Polish for "wasp" (or "Vespa"), the Osa scooter moved the masses with its hefty 149-cc, 3.25x14-millimeter engine. Only since the Iron Curtain fell have East Bloc scooters crossed the line into the West. Scooter novelties like this M50 Osa made by the Fabryka Motocykli of Poland are the find of a lifetime for the avid collector.

Scooters are a social appliance. While automobiles shield people from the outside world, putt-putts open up new horizons with the opportunity to meet new people. Soon piazzas and coffee shops were buzzing with scooterists, and as the *New Yorker* warned in 1957, "This is more than a fad, it's a revolution, and I don't see how anything can stop it."

Romance on two-wheels sprang eternal as scooterists were dying to meet each other. "Sports riders in this country are mostly either single or newly marrieds (scooters are so conducive to romance that there is a fast turnover between these categories)," according to a 1957 *Popular Science* article.

Social scooter protocol was strict. "It's an unwritten code for scooterists to greet each other," said a Vespa rider in the *New York Times Magazine* in

The ultimate mod machine was the souped-up Turismo Veloce 175 Series II with extra mirrors and lights attached to the mandatory roll bar. This second series of TV Lambrettas raised the headlamp to the handlebars to follow the turning wheel. Rather than updating the unreliable TV Series I engine, Innocenti bored out the popular Li motor, making a 8.6-horsepower engine of 62x58 millimeter. The TV would again follow the Li's lead in 1962 with the slimline styling of the 1960s.

1958. If a scooterist saw a broken-down putt-putt on the side of the road, proper etiquette required assistance even if the passing rider had never even looked under the side panels before.

Prejudices that grated motorcyclists were inevitably applied toward scooterists who tried their best to prove that they weren't the "Wild Ones." The *New York Times Magazine* backed them up in 1957 claiming that "Scooterists emphasize that they drive for pleasure, not for speed." The *New Yorker* defended the straight-laced scooterists as well, describing putt-putt owners as "quietly dressed, sober-looking scooterists of both sexes and a variety of ages darting amiably, by day and night, through the thick of midtown traffic."

Since scooters broke the ice between riders, clubs formed and met to discuss their *raison d'être*. "What are the club's purposes?" a scooterist queried in a 1956 *New Yorker* article. "Thinking up scooter trips, getting discounts on spare parts, lobbying for the abolition of such laws as the one that keeps us off parkways."

The first Vespa Club was established by Adolf Nass in 1951 in Saarbrucken, Germany, with none of the existential angst but all of the Teutonic organization typically associated with things German. More than 300 scooter clubs were then formed around the world with 1,200 accredited Vespa service stations worldwide to fix putt-putts in distress. Newsletters such as *Vespa News*, *Lambretta Leader*, and *Jet-Set* were translated into numerous languages for the loyal scooter legions.

Eschewing the bench racing and beer drinking of many motorcycle clubs, scooterists instead did things like set up "Gymkhana" obstacle courses to prove their riding agility. A 1959 Cushman comic book delved into Gymkhana's origin, "Historians believe the British started them in India. Mounted horsemen of the Bengal Lancers sharpened battle maneuvers by wheeling and turning through obstacles." Inspiration to hop on a Cushman and practice war maneuvers.

By the late 1950s, scooter sports such as putt-putt polo had already been played for a couple of decades. *Popular Mechanics* in 1939 described the "sport" as, "A bit faster than bicycle polo, the motorized sport brings occasional spectacular spills, but it's easy to jump off and the injuries to players are few."

Scooter Raids

The newfound freedom that comes with two wheels coaxed scooterists off of the Gymkhana courses to attempt to climb mountains, traverse continents, and even attach pontoons and cross the English Channel. Cross-country putt-putt endurance tests were called "raids," and naturally

Continuing the pilot-scooter connection begun by Amelia Earhart, aviator hero Colonel Roscoe Turner opened one of the first Salsbury scooter dealerships. His mere presence at the San Diego shop would generate a crowd. Though the opening was in early 1936, the rally-goers are riding the new 1937 Model De Luxe Motor Glides. E. Foster Salsbury archives

As publicity stunts, scooter manufacturers staged cross-country "raids" to show the world how reliable their two-stroke wonders could be. Here, founder E. Foster Salsbury checks the gas level in a Salsbury Model 85 in the late 1940s, so this Canadian importer isn't stranded halfway to Vancouver. E. Foster Salsbury archives

created splendid publicity opportunities for scooter makers. When news spread that a Vespa had climbed Snowdon Mountain in England, that a group of Lambrettas had traveled from London to Milan nonstop, or that a Vespisti had braved the cold in a raid to the Arctic Circle, scooter popularity further soared. Scooterists on raids became missionaries, their angelic wings a flashy scoot with a pillion seat.

Innocenti realized that loyal Lambrettisti traveling the world would do more to promote their scooters than advertising ever could. Scooters became Lambretta's way to unite the world. A 1950s Innocenti advertising campaign called "The Whole World of Lambretta" tried to break down national boundaries, making the scooter the ultimate unifier as it "showed scooters posed against Buddhist temples or busy London streets," according to Hebdige. In a 1954 Innocenti advertising film, *Travel Far, Travel Wide*, the voice-over said, "A frontier. And on the other side, a completely different way of life. But whatever country you go to in the world today, you'll find Lambrettas and Lambretta service stations."

The ultimate scooter raid—easily beating Magellan's record—was the 'round the world trip executed on a 1954 Mustang. American Dick Miller circumnavigated the globe armed only with extra inner tubes, fuel tanks, an American flag, and "USA" written everywhere on his scooter. Miller's scooter truly shrunk distances and brought people together around the world.

Shriner Stunts

In the United States, the scooter show inevitably revolved around the town festival with fez-topped Shriners performing dangerously slow figure-eight maneuvers on Cushman scooters while tossing taffy to the tots. Rockers had their Triumphs, Hell's Angels their Harleys, Mods their Lambrettas, and Shriners their Cushmans.

The Masonic pact with scooterdom was signed by Shriner Bill Ammon, son of Cushman's intrepid leader Charles Ammon, who convinced the company to offer a special Shriner scooter in 1957. Leather fringe and shiny rivets helped show off the steeds as did chrome widgets including horns, safety bars, floorboards, seat rails, locking gas caps, and fender tips. In an attempt to steal the Masonic market from Cushman, Vespa offered special Shriner accessories.

Today Shriners can even be spotted on Honda scooters, but Masons will always be *semper fi* to Cushman Eagles.

In Mod We Trust

London's lower-class East End launched the Mod rebellion. Teenagers with a little extra loot in their pockets from part-time jobs hit the classy shops on Carnaby Street for the latest Italian styles to one-up their mates. Rather than rejecting consumption like so many other youth movements before, materialism was the Mod cry. Each object purchased became a fashion statement and object of rebellion. Mods took formal fashion to the extreme by being far better dressed than even uptight upper-class fops. Mods were a "grotesque parody of the aspirations of [their] parents . . . who used goods as weapons of exclusion," according to historian Hebdige.

Mods studied the latest magazines and tuned in religiously to *Ready, Steady, Go!*, a TV show that featured the "with-it" bands of the week from The Small Faces to the Hollies, including an opening shot of a scooter. Bored stiff during the week, Mods counted the hours to the weekend, and when the whistle blew, two-stroke scooter exhaust filled the air and the dance halls rocked with Northern Soul.

Mods popped "blues" and other amphetamines to keep Monday at bay as long as possible. In typical "reefer madness" hype, the *Sunday Mirror* ran a feature in 1964, "Exposing the Drug Menace," with a large photo of a Drinamyl pill bottle. The article stated, "They began by experimenting with purple hearts

During the 1950s, European scooter rallies often dressed up participants in cowboy and Indian garb and placed the poor souls on a scooter—in this case a French Gillet (Bernardet) 51. François-Marie Dumas archives

At the annual Vespa meeting in Paris, these lunaires, or "moon men," impressed the world with their stylish yellow outfits. The latest 1956 Vespas are under most of the get ups, but who knows what's underneath the flying saucer in the rear? Hans Kruger archives

and other pep-pills, then progress via 'reefers' (marijuana) to heroin and cocaine—the two drugs that almost always lead to death before the age of 35."

In Dick Hebdige's *Subculture*, he wrote, "pills medically prescribed for the treatment of neuroses were used as ends-in-themselves, and the motor scooter, originally an ultra-respectable means of transport, was turned into a menacing symbol of group solidarity."

Vespa-Lambretta Wars

The essential Mod fashion accessory was the scooter, preferably a Lambretta or Vespa. Piaggio's scooters had been the first to cross the English Channel when the Douglas motorcycle firm began importing Vespas in 1949. While Mods wouldn't latch on to the smooth Italian styling of Vespas for a few years, the stage was nevertheless set for the Lambretta-Vespa wars.

Innocenti's scooters invaded England when the Agg family set up a huge distribution network with a massive marketing campaign and many more dealers and repair shops than Douglas Vespa. Rather than constructing a factory to actually stamp out scooters in the United Kingdom, though, the Agg family wisely cashed in on the "Made in Italy" status. Anything Italian was vogue, or as Hebdige wrote of the Mods, "He is English by birth, Italian by choice."

Douglas Vespas usually were quite a bit cheaper than the latest Lambrettas, because the models weren't updated annually as retooling the British

By creating a movement rather than merely a product, Vespa developed brand loyalty with aficionados pushing Piaggio more than any PR shill ever could. The Piaggio magazine spread the word of upcoming rallies, marriages on Vespas, scooter raids around Europe, and, of course, any new products on the market. Hans Kruger archives

factory every year would stymie profits. Piaggio showrooms stocked only a few of the imported, speedy GS scooters since they were more expensive to ship rather than selling a home-bred Douglas Vespa.

Lambrettas earned a reputation as the faster of the two scooters, since scooter shop window displays—exclusively showing one make or the other—featured only the quickest, latest models, often the Lambretta TV 175 Series 2 (not the Series 1 lemon). Unwilling to go softly into that good night, the Piaggio company released its gorgeous GS 160 Vespa in 1962, the pinnacle of Vespadom. In 1963, Innocenti responded to the British market and the Isle of Man scooter races with the TV 200 (a.k.a. GT 200). This provoked Piaggio's SS120, then Innocenti's SX200 and so on as the two scooter giants battled back and forth for market supremacy.

While Piaggio and Innocenti scrabbled for more horsepower, most Mods focused their attention on the attachment of any accessory they could screw onto their scooters. A British ad for scooter accessories said in huge letters, "Go Gay!" and featured a Lambretta decked out with flags, plaid seat covers, a windscreen, plaid saddlebags, and every piece of chrome that could fit. "[A]ll these extras would slow the bike down considerably, although this didn't bother Mods as speed wasn't their priority, the slower you go, the more people see you," according to the Mod handbook *Empire Made*. Certain accessories were deemed "cool" while others were quickly consigned to the dustbin. Oversized windscreens and flags were passé one moment, while chrome crashbars, lights, and mirrors were hip the next.

Two-tone styling came to scooters via Eddy Grimstead's shop on Barking Road in London. Soon Innocenti offered standard two-tone paint schemes to the British market, and each dealer offered its own styling with names like "Imperial," "Hurricane," "Z-Type," and "Mona."

While the average Mod could scarcely afford to spring for a new scoot every year, a few simple tricks ensured a state of the art scooter, at least in looks. For example, last year's Lambretta panels could easily be swapped for this year's panels. Even the notoriously unreliable Lambretta TV Series 1 were purchased and then made to look like new with a bench seat, chrome accessories and the latest side panels,. Since almost all scooter keys were identical, a black market scooter trade soon flourished in London with faked upscale scooters running rampant.

Rockers' Rebellion

"Hey Johnny, what are you rebelling against?"
"Whatta ya got?"
—Marlon Brando in *The Wild One*.

While Mods were busy exchanging styling cues and twisting to Northern Soul, their arch-enemies, the Rockers, were dropping a shilling in the Ace Café jukebox, kick starting their café racers, and making the rounds before the song ended. The lines were drawn and teenagers had to choose which side they were on. "You've got to be either a Mod or a Rocker to mean anything," a Mod explained to a reporter from one of Britain's tabloids in 1964.

The dawn of the Rockers can be traced back to "American motorcycling's day of infamy" in Hollister, California, in 1947. In the aftermath of a race weekend run amuck, a *Time/Life* photographer staged a photo of a member of the Booze Fighters club on a Harley surrounded by emptied beer bottles, and an incident was born. The public was outraged. How could motorcycles that had provided such patriotic service during the war be transformed into a tool of rebellion? Hollywood cashed in on the perceived menace, with 1953's *The Wild One*. In trying to understand the rebels, Cathy (the pretty square) prods Johnny (Marlon Brando):

Cathy: "What do you do? I mean, do you just ride around or do you go on some sort of picnic or something?"
Johnny: "A picnic? Man, you are too square. I have to straighten you out. Now listen, you don't go any one special place, that's cornball style. You just go!

On March 19, 1954, the Cortile del Castello in Turin was inundated with 485 Vespas to show the heavens the Piaggio logo for the annual Motoraduno Nazionale. Christa Solbach archives

Mods decked out their scooters with every bell and whistle that they could slap on. Unfortunately, scooter bandits spoiled the fun when they began prying off the metallic plaques, leaving the poor putt-putts buck naked.

[snaps his fingers]. A bunch gets together after all week. It builds up. The idea is to have a ball. Now, if you gonna stay cool, you gotta wail. You gotta put something down. You gotta make some jive. Don't you know what I'm talking about?"

Just as the Mods studied magazines and movies to perfect their style, the British Rockers carefully copied the American movement, adding typical English flair. In Johnny Stuart's great testament *Rockers*, he describes the style, "Then comes the scarf. . . . It was stolen from American cowboy movies . . . the Rocker begins to take on something of the cowboy's identity as a wanderer, tramp, hobo; a bit of a villain, too."

Mod disdain for Rockers was summed up by 17-year-old Terry Gordon as quoted in the *Daily Mirror* in 1964: "Rockers look like Elvis Presley, only worse. Mod girls don't wear any make-up—only foundation. Rocker girls use a lot of bright pink lipstick and piles of make-up."

The Battle of Brighton

The year 1964 was a banner year for delinquency. In California, the Attorney General released a notorious—and mostly fabricated—report on "Hoodlum Activities" and what to look for in a "hood." According to the report, rebels had "an embroidered patch of a winged skull wearing a motorcycle helmet. . . . Many affect beards and their hair is usually long and unkempt. Some wear a single earring in a pierced ear lobe. . . . Some clubs provide that initiates shall be tattooed. . . . Another patch worn by some members bears the number '13.'"

Across the Atlantic, Innocenti was innocently planning a picnic. Any self-respecting Mod kick-started the Lammie, and hit the beaches of Brighton for a bank holiday in May. So, too, did the Rockers. "We will fight them on the beach!" became the Churchill-mocking rallying cry as amphetamine-fueled Mods clashed with their nemeses, the Rockers. Deck chairs and punches flew amidst unsuspecting sunbathers, as the Mods and Rockers dueled, the bobbies tried to subdue them, and the tabloids smiled, knowing they had secured tomorrow's headline.

Innocenti and Piaggio were horrified as their docile scooters became a tool of the revolution. Needless to say, they refrained from sponsoring future scooter outings in the United Kingdom. "The words 'social scootering' had formerly summoned up the image of orderly mass rallies. Now it was suddenly linked to a more sinister collective: An army of youth, ostensibly conformist—barely distinguishable as individuals from each other or

Kids, don't try this at home! Piaggio decided to take Gymkhana obstacle courses to a new level by having an official acrobat team show off the versatility of the incredible Vespa. Soon becoming a regular feature to awed Italian TV watchers, Innocenti had to chime in with its own stunt team fitting more than 14 riders on a single Lambretta. The pictured reenactment of the Vespa team shows one rider with a modern full-face helmet, obviously not a true believer in their ability. Wolfgang Roucka

the crowd—and yet capable of concerted acts of vandalism," wrote Hebdige in *Hiding in the Light*.

2nd and 3rd Mod Movements

Some social historians, like Dick Hebdige, mourned the "death" of the Mods in the 1970s. "Somewhere on the way home from school or work, the mods went 'missing': they were absorbed into a 'noonday underground' of cellar clubs, discotheques, boutiques and record shops which lay hidden beneath the 'straight world.'" If only Hebdige would have searched a little harder, he would have found the Mod chameleon had just moved on to the next style, though still atop a scooter.

In the late 1970s, the film version of the Who's reenactment of the infamous Mod-Rocker wars, *Quadrophenia*, rang true for a new generation of Mods. Suddenly, two-stroke scooter exhaust again battled four-stroke motorcycles for dominance of London's cobblestones. This new wave rejected once-popular Mod bands like the Rolling Stones, the Kinks, and the Who as greasy Rockers, and instead latched on to a music style imported from Jamaica, known as Ska, Dub Reggae, and Rock Steady. "Two-tone" came to be the new Mod description since it described the checkered patterns of clothes, two-tone scooters (harking back to the original Mod invasion), the legendary record label releasing the best Ska, and the idea of black and white, Jamaican and British, coming together to produce the best music of the late 1970s and early 1980s.

In 1995, *The Independent*, a daily English newspaper, declared that a "British Mod wave" had hit the runways from Milan to London. Fashion designer Anna Sui placed Linda Evangelista on a vintage Lambretta and pushed her out onto the runway.

In spite of what fickle designers say is "in" this minute, Mod style, music, and especially scooters has never been so widespread as evidenced by more Ska bands than ever before. The scooter renaissance and subculture boasts more aficionados than during the dawn of Mod culture on Carnaby Street.

While some Mods decked out their ride, others preferred the classic, sleek Italian lines of the original scooter. This 1966 Vespa Primavera (or spring) with pillion seat could zip the sharp Mod with the latest bobbed haircut to the dance hall or to the beach for a bank holiday.

PUTT-PUTT POLICE

Greenwich Villagers of the swinging sixties dubbed scooter police "buzzy fuzzy" as the two-stroke enforcers zipped around Washington Square trying to nab outlaws. In 1967, *Time* poked fun at "the sight of beefy cops on dainty putt-putts," explaining that "the putt-putting noise daunts would-be lawbreakers; the potential speed (60 mph) and mobility enable wheezy cops to outrun juvenile delinquents." Perhaps *Time* laughed, but muggings dropped 30 percent in Central Park and 40 percent in Prospect Park thanks to these "Fuzz with a Buzz."

California had C.H.I.P.s for motorcycle dragnets, New York had S.C.R.A.M.B.L.E. patrols, or Scooters in Communication with Range and Mobility for Better Law Enforcement. The cops "linked by radio communication, ordinarily patrol slowly to create a continual and visible deterrent to criminal activity." By 1966, the NYPD zipped around on 59 Vespas and *American City Magazine* heralded the scooter as the cure to Gotham's grief, "The foot patrolman—a lonely fellow—must check into the precinct from a call box once every hour. The same man, mounted on a scooter, can signal instantly for help and can rely on the quick scramble response of his scooter team-mates in the precinct. A scooter patrolman is never alone."

Chapter 6 — Scooter World Domination

While European and American scooter makers were concentrating on style, Japan was busy building the most practical and reliable scoots the world had ever seen. The Fuji Rabbit was the first to make the scene in 1946, matching Piaggio's timetable on the other side of the globe, and borrowing heavily from the 1930s American scooter revolution. While only eight of the 135-cc four-stroke-powered Fujis were born that year, the Rabbits multiplied into slick steeds in the 1950s with rounded design, long wheelbase, and peppy 125-cc engines. The luxury Fuji S-61 and the Superflow followed Honda's footsteps in the 1960s and tried to compete with the larger maker's ubiquitous Cub moped.

Piaggio still lived on the cutting edge when the "New Vespa" cruised into the piazza, this one parked in Rome. Italians were split. How could Piaggio improve on a classic? The design harks back to the height of scooterdom when BSA and British Triumph teamed up to produce the Tigress/Sunbeam scooter in 1959, alas at the end of the scooter boom. While Corradino d'Ascanio's muse inspired him to create the first Vespa in 1945, "All the designers were trying to get their name on the new Vespa," said a young Piaggio designer in 1997.

Another Japanese giant, Mitsubishi gave up production of its Zero-San fighter planes, seeing little future in the kamikaze market, and wisely opted for the scooter field with its chunky-looking C-11 Pigeon. Within a few years, a designer's touch turned the Pigeon into the sleek Silver Pigeon that became one of the mainstays of the Japanese market. The Mitsubishi marque reminded American vets of the controversial Pacific arena, so when Rockford of Illinois imported Pigeons, it conveniently covered the Japanese emblem with its own. In the late 1950s, Montgomery Ward bought out Rockford, renaming the scooters "Riverside" and appending tropical model names like Nassau, Miami, and Waikiki.

The little putt-putt company that could, however, was Honda, producing more mopeds/scooters than any other company in the world. The son of a blacksmith, Soichiro Honda's immediate postwar production talents would range from piston rings to airplane propellers to motorized bicycles. The year 1947 saw the Model A moped built by 13 employees in a small, 12x18-foot shed. In 1953, the Cub clip-on engine was born from this original Model A design, resulting in the Cub scooter that proliferated around the world with more than 15

89

million built. In addition to these omnipresent moped/scooter wannabes, Honda also produced space-age scooters with bizarre chrome air ducts and styling perfect for any *Blade Runner* android. The June KA, powered by a 189-cc overhead valve engine, was the first, in 1954. The KB, with a 220-cc, 9-horsepower motor, followed in 1955. The world wasn't ready for these glossy mounts, though, choosing instead Honda's more practical mini putt-putts.

Now Suzuki, Yamaha, and Honda are neck and neck with stunning lineups of plastic scooters. Only a handful of models venture beyond Asia, but even these are enough to give European manufacturers an inferiority complex.

Scooter Jetpads of the Future

"It is the business of the future to be dangerous," according to historian A. N. Whitehead. But nowadays scooters are fairly safe when compared to the early gadabouts. The new models have a look of pure speed with angular lines mimicking today's sport bikes.

At the beginning of the twenty-first century, the majority of scooter manufacturing has moved from Europe and the United States to Asia. India makes Lambrettas, and Japan produces more Honda scooters than any other scooter in the world. Two-stroke engines sheathed with metal or plastic bodies clog the streets of the East. Even staid *Consumer's Digest* gave these scoots rave reviews in 1994:

When Piaggio decided to "retire" the Vespa and replace it with a plasticized version, dubbed the Cosa or "Thing," the end seemed near. The Cosa was a modern update complete with 12-volt electrics and three speedy models, the 125 cc, 150 cc, and 200 cc. Even though parts were interchangeable with the Vespa, the public couldn't stand the pseudonym and demanded their old classic. Piaggio quickly backtracked and re-released the Vespa to crowds of well-wishers. Can you say Coke Classic?

Of all Piaggio's plastic scooters that have appeared and broken, the Sfera's friendly and futuristic curves made it a bestseller as the lowly cousin of the Vespa. With a smaller but well-tuned engine, it could easily zip by a classic GS with half as much noise, giving scooterists carte blanche to enter pedestrian-only zones. This Sfera was spotted outside Milan's Castello Sforzesco.

The P-Series Vespas revolutionized Piaggio and kept them in the scooter-making ball game while Innocenti filed for the Italian equivalent of Chapter 11. Updates such as a separate oil reservoir (for when gas stations are plumb out of miscela premixed gas), turn signals, and overall reliability made the new line of Vespas the trade standard. The year after the P-series' debut in 1978, Piaggio took over Moto Gilera and began producing competition to the Vespa in-house.
Michael Dregni

As the premier plastic scooter, Yamaha Riva runs rampant across Asia. "When a car is just too much!" to squeeze down side streets and park anywhere. The Riva has crossed the ocean and hit the U.S. market by storm while Italian scooters ran away with their collective tails between their legs in fear of product liability suits. This 1998 "fun little get about (sic)" or gadabout, comes in two engine sizes, 125 cc pictured, and 49 cc with three models, the Razz, Jog, and Zuma. Yamaha

"These fuel-miserly vehicles are nicer than ever for urban commuting and, though subject to various licensing limitations, good for kids not quite old enough to drive a car."

While scooter manufacturers often look back for styling cues, they seem to know that futurist Marshall McLuhan was right when he said, "The future of the future is the present." Groundbreakers like the original Autoped, E. Foster Salsbury's Motor Glide, and d'Ascanio's Vespa ignored what the market supposedly wanted and went with a dream of the future. Nostalgic scooters like Aprilia Scarabeo, Italjet Velocifero, and the Honda Shadow take the best of both worlds: classic styling and reliable, modern engines.

Now in the design laboratories of Piaggio in Pontedera, a young team of designers from France, Sweden, and Italy are hashing out the future of scootering with bizarre drawings, most of which will never get beyond the prototype stage. Even BMW seems interested in the scooter realm and has shown prototypes of what it calls the C1, a fully covered, ultramodern scoot.

To step into the future, history must be ignored. "We want no part of it, the past," according to Marinetti who knew that to invent anything new, thousands of years of history needs to be put on the shelf. Taking the futurist's cue, manufacturers have been copying the sleek, triangular designs employed on modern sport bikes. But while today's scooters look space age, their power plants have evolved little from the Autoped of the 1910s. This is changing, though, as new sound and emissions regulations push engine designers to experiment with high-density electric batteries and other alternate power sources to propel the next generation of putt-putts.

Clogged cities are banning cars in the center to lower emissions, leaving business people to hop on

Part Goldwing part Lambretta, the 1998 FB-S Future Concept Design scooter by Honda practically floats down the streets of Tokyo. This futuristic E-Z Boy prototype comes hot on the tail of the outrageous success of Honda's top-of-the-line Helix scooters. The 250 cc Helix could easily reach 65 miles per hour, and this new space-age motorcycle-cum-scooter could leave Helix loungers in the dust. Honda

Made from the original Vespa molds that were sold to India and bought back by Italjet, the 49-cc Velocifero hit the market by storm with Piaggio unable to sue for copyright since it had sold the rights years prior. Italjet then beat Piaggio to the punch again by fearlessly attacking the U.S. market, being the sole new Italian scooter on American roads. Proclaimed one of Vogue's "10 Most Wanted," with text saying it's the "wheels of choice for hip Brits like the band Oasis," ignoring the fact that Oasis singer Liam Gallagher brags about his metal Zündapp Bella. Regardless of what scooter purists claim is the pinnacle of scooterdom, styling's return to the putt-putt heydays of yore in the form of the Velocifero, the Scarabeo, and the Nuova Vespa is a promise of good scooters to come. Susan Sacher

their two-strokes to zip down to the financial district. While scooters were mere teenage playthings in the 1960s, at the dawn of the twenty-first century they are now embraced by some adults as a viable alternative to the automobile.

Attitudes change, but the scooter still retains its basic shape, "even when it is powered by a mini nuclear reactor or as a vehicle to drive on the moon" as Vespa designer Corradino d'Ascanio put it. And perhaps that is the best testament to the simple power of this timeless two-wheeled design.

ROMAN HOLIDAY REVISITED

Cary Grant and Audrey Hepburn did more for the cause of scootering in one short jaunt through Rome's piazzas than any other single event. Scooting through modern Rome, however, is like going to war. Revisiting Rome recently, a few unwritten rules of riding came to light:

1. **Always go as fast as possible.** If you don't have your scooter floored, folks will wonder what's wrong with your ride.

2. **Street signs are mere suggestions.** "One-way signs are intended for cars," scooterists will tell you. Follow them into an onslaught of traffic. If you're worried about getting a ticket, just follow the pack of Vespas, Velociferos, and Scarabeos, and there's no way the police will be able to pull over all the insubordinate scooterists. Besides, the police go the wrong way, too.

3. **Obstacles are to be overcome.** *American City Magazine* wrote in 1966 that "Scooters evade barriers, jump over traffic islands, cut through parks, bump down hills or steps, and slice through narrow openings." The same applies for modern Rome. Asking any native for directions will yield helpful hints like "Just go right up on the sidewalk, through the public garden." If you protest saying it's illegal to drive there, the inevitable response is, "Oh no, with a Vespa you can go there." Just don't get caught.

4. **Ignore other drivers.** If motorists see you notice them, they know that you will stop and avoid hitting them. This is the scooterist's blind leap of faith. Just go forth, the sea of traffic will part.

5. **The world is your parking lot**. The same applies for modern Rome as applied for the Big Apple, stated in a *New Yorker* article from 1957, "You can park scooters almost anywhere without getting a ticket. In a metered area, the usual thing is to park them sidewise, between two parked cars. In theory, a scooter hasn't any right to be there, but the police

Lambretta

seem to overlook it. Truth is, nobody seems to mind what scooters do." Take advantage of it. If by some bizarre happenstance you do get a ticket, or *multa*, ignore it.

6. **Traffic lights are decoration.** If you have a red, it's merely a warning that you may have to dodge cars coming from the side. Or as a Roman cabbie said, "Scooterists are all color blind."

7. **No cop, no stop.** "In Rome there are many laws, so you can pick and choose which ones to follow," any Roman will quickly tell you. *Polizia* in *Campo de' Fiori* wag their index finger to warn off scooters from the pedestrian-only square, only to see the same scooter zip through the piazza from a different entrance.

8. **Use your size.** A scooter may not be able to pass a Lamborghini Diablo on a Monza race track, but in Roman traffic, just sneak between the legions of creeping cars passing through the triumphal arches. Nothing gets the goat of a Ferrari driver like a Lambretta leaving him in the dust. Even *Popular Science* back in 1957 agreed, "In heavy traffic you can retaliate by nuzzling in along stalled cars and chugging ahead . . . the scooter, a deft and agile machine, can pick its way through vacation-time traffic tangles like a chipmunk through a wood pile."

9. **Chatting on your cell phone.** Driving a scooter usually requires two hands to control the gears, clutch, and gas, making talking on your *telefonino* an art that requires the skill of a gymnast. If you've no one to call, light up a cigarette using your third hand.

10. **Making *una bella figura*.** Always act as if someone is watching, but never pay them mind. If no one really notices you, try this old trick: whip out a hacksaw and cut off the last few inches of your tailpipe for some further volume. To avoid ruining your *bella figura* when your damn two-stroke engine kills again, pretend that this spot was exactly where you meant to stop. Remember, the only time your scooter can break down is in a secluded spot with a member of the opposite sex.

Appendix
Essential Reading

Barnes, Richard. *Mods!* London: Eel Pie Publishing, 1979.

Biancalana, Stefano, and Marchianò, Michele. *La Vespa . . . e Tutti i Suoi Vespini.* Milano: Giorgio Nada Editore, 1995.

Boldrini, Maurizio, and Calabrese, Omar. *il libro della Comumicazione.* Pontedera: Piaggio Veicoli Europei S.p.A., 1995.

Brockway, Eric. Vespa: *An Illustrated History.* Sparkford, England: Haynes Publications, 1993.

Calabrese, Omar. *The Cult of the Vespa.* Pontedera: Piaggio Veicoli Europei S.p.A., 1996.

Cox, Nigel. *Lambretta Innocenti: An Illustrated History.* Sparkford, England: Haynes Publications, 1996.

Dregni, Michael & Eric. *Illustrated MotorScooter Buyer's Guide.* Osceola, Wisconsin: Motorbooks International, 1993.

Dregni, Michael & Eric. *Scooters!* Osceola, Wisconsin: Motorbooks International, 1995.

Dumas, François-Marie, and Didier, Ganneau. *Scooters du Monde: 100 Ans d'Histoire.* Paris: Éditions E/P/A, 1995.

Fanfani, Tommaso. *Una Leggenda Verso il Futuro: I Centodieci Anni di Storia della Piaggio.* Pontedera: Piaggio Veicoli Europei, 1994.

Gerald, Michael. *Mustang: A Different Breed of Steed.* N.p.: self-published, n.d.

Goyard, Jean, and Pascal, Dominique. *Tous les scooters du monde.* Paris: Éditions Ch. Massin, 1988.

Goyard, Jean, Pascal, Dominique, and Salvat, Bernard. *Vespa Histoire et Technique.* Paris Éditions Moto Legende/ Rétroviseur, 1992.

Hebdige, Dick. "Object as Image: The Italian Scooter Cycle" *Hiding in the Light.* London and New York: Routledge, 1988.

Kubisch, Ulrich, ed. *Deutsche Motorroller 1949–73.* München, Germany: Schrader Automobil-Bücher, 1992.

Lintelmann, Reinhard. *Deutsche Roller und Kleinwagen der Fünfziger Jahre.* Brilon, Germany: Podszun Motor-Bücher, 1986.

Pascal, Dominique. *Scooters de chez nous.* Boulogne, France: Éditions MDM, 1993.

Rawlings, Terry, and Badman, Keith. *Empire Made: The Handy Parka Pocket Guide to All Things Mod!* London: Complete Music Publications, 1997.

Rivola, Luigi. *Chi Vespa Mangia le Mele: Storia della Vespa.* Milano: Giorgio Nada Editore, 1993.

Roos, Peter. *Vespa Stracciatella: Ein Lust- und Bilderbuch von der italienischen Beweglichkeit.* Berlin: Transit Buchverlag, 1985.

Somerville, Bill. *The Complete Guide to Cushman Motor Scooters.* Ponca City, Oklahoma: Cushman Pub., 1988.

Struss, Dieter. *Vespa.* Augsburg: Battenberg Verlag, 1995.

Stuart, Johnny. *Rockers!* London: Plexus Publishing Ltd. 1987.

Tessera, Vittorio. *Innocenti Lambretta.* Milano: Giorgio Nada Editore, 1995.

Webster, Michael. *Motor Scooters.* Haverfordwest, England: Shire Publications, Ltd., 1986.

Zeichner, Walter, ed. *Vespa Motorroller 1948–1986.* München, Germany: Schrader Automobil-Bücher, 1987.

Index